What people are saying about

An Anthropology of Nothing in Particular

This is a beautifully written piece of work – it deals with the kind of existential concerns that anthropology normally deals with so badly by approaching them through thickets of deep theory that all too often become the focus of attention rather than the questions of being that such theory is allegedly intended to illuminate. Instead, the author takes the direct route of explaining in clear and simple – yet never simplistic – terms, why an endless quest for meaning may carry downsides and blindsides if relentlessly pursued.

Keir Martin, author of *The Deat[...] [...]e Big Shots*

It is a rare pleasure to read ab[...] [...]th the constant notion of wanting to read more about nothing! The chapters of this book meander around nothing, leading the reader back and forth between observations of a place in its non-existence and detailed being, references to and analysis of nothingness versus nothing and the importance of a counterpart of nothing in everything. Like with its contents the author transforms language into a form of questions and in between – is it poetry? Is it theory? – contesting blind spots in a kaleidoscopic manner. A text one reads so fast just to start over again when through in order to not have gotten lost on any of the details.

Katharina Stadler, conceptual artist and independent scholar

Frederiksen's book is a well-written and very interesting anthropological experiment. Not only does it address meaninglessness and the challenge it poses to the venerated tradition of looking for meaning and structure behind all kinds of everyday phenomena and personal life stories, Frederiksen also searches for a style of representation (or perhaps rather presentation) that resonates with his object of study. I really appreciate the way he takes his informants literally, not only in the sense of taking them seriously. Boldly and with success, he employs literary means in order to describe how nothing in particular takes place among them.

Anne Line Dalsgaard, author of *Matters of Life and Longing*

Also by the author

Georgian Portraits – Essays on the Afterlives of a Revolution. Zero Books, 2017 (with Katrine B. Gotfredsen).

ISBN: 978-1-78535-362-8

An Anthropology
of Nothing
in Particular

An Anthropology
of Nothing
in Particular

Martin Demant Frederiksen

Winchester, UK
Washington, USA

First published by Zero Books, 2018
Zero Books is an imprint of John Hunt Publishing Ltd., No. 3 East St., Alresford,
Hampshire SO24 9EE, UK
office1@jhpbooks.net
www.johnhuntpublishing.com
www.zero-books.net

For distributor details and how to order please visit the 'Ordering' section on our website.

Text copyright: Martin Demant Frederiksen 2017

ISBN: 978 1 78535 699 5
978 1 78535 700 8 (ebook)
Library of Congress Control Number: 2017953140

A CIP catalogue record for this book is available from the British Library.

Design: Cecilia Perriard

Printed and bound by CPI Group (UK) Ltd, Croydon, CR0 4YY, UK

We operate a distinctive and ethical publishing philosophy in
all areas of our business, from our global network of authors to
production and worldwide distribution.

CONTENTS

To Pelle, Neel and Ene

PREFACE

Something missing is missing

Terrence W. Deacon, Incomplete Nature

BLINDSPOT

In short, this is an exploration of what goes missing when one looks for meaning. And although this in many ways is not a book that is as such obsessed with clarification, an initial one might be in place. Namely, the interrelation of nihilism, nothingness and meaninglessness that forms my point of departure. There are many definitions of what nihilism is or can be, and a vast literature exploring different angles and conceptualizations of the notion.[1] Although he neither coined the term nor was alone in depicting it, it is likely to be the work of Friedrich Nietzsche that first comes to mind when hearing about nihilism. The specter of nihilism for Nietzsche had risen through a decline of values, an enervation of the will. Nietzsche's solution was to accelerate this condition through an active or radical nihilism, as opposed to a passive form of nihilism, in order to create new values.[2] As read by Deleuze, passive nihilism may be seen as "a world without values", whereas its opposite radical nihilism is a situation of "values without a world".[3]

On a descriptive level, this book departs from characters most closely resembling the former, with sentiments often aligning with the character Pechorin in the Lermontov novel *A Hero of Our Time*; one that is likely to have inspired Nietszche in his writings on nihilism.[4] The novel presents context and situations full of action but where, for those partaking in this reality, nothing is perceived as happening. In the words of Bulent Diken, "a constellation in which nothing is held absolute and everything is subjected to critique".[5] In the pages to come, we are thus not dealing with the kind of political activism that for instance surrounded the Russian nihilist movements of the

1

1860s[6], but rather with displays of nihilist sentiments. For that reason, I therefore follow Simon Critchley, via Nietzsche and Samuel Beckett, in seeing nihilism here as a crisis of meaning and distrust in endpoints.[7]

There have been claims that meaninglessness has become epidemic in the contemporary world, one perceived consequence of this being that people increasingly turn against both society and political establishments with little concern for the content (or lack of content) that might follow. As such, despite the fact that encounters with meaninglessness, nihilism and nothingness are often seen as troubling there is reason not to be blind towards the presence and actual consequences of meaninglessness, and to turn away from seeing these phenomena or notions only as troubling but also as factual realities. The "hedonistic nihilism" noted by Mark Fisher in *Capitalist Realism* is revealing in this context: a world where imagining political alternatives becomes increasingly difficult and action therefore comes to seem pointless.[8] In many ways, the present book departs from this type of situation and seeks to depict from within. As such, it is a book that gravitates towards nothing. It does not do so through a standard linear narrative (that would betray its contents) but through interwoven snapshots, scenes and fabulations.

Stanley Rosen has argued that nihilism is primarily a theoretical and only secondarily a practical or cultural phenomen.[9] The question is then, how we may approach instances in which nihilism, nothingness and meaninglessness do in fact exist as components of social life. Social sciences are typically centered on conveying some form of coherence and meaningfulness[10] and as a consequence, nothingness and pointlessness may easily come to stand forth as a challenge. Hence, a form of radical nihilism will perhaps make itself present now and again, mainly in the shape of invitations to consider radical alternatives on the level of theory, analysis and writing, paraphrasing respectively Ghassan Hage and Joao Biehl either as forms of radical imagination or as alternative figures of thought.[11] Lisa Stevenson, in *Life Beside Itself*, has called for seeing what cannot be clearly understood as a legitimate ethnographic object, and for being attentive to moments when facts falter in the shadows of discursive certainties. Her method of doing so is aiming at an imagistic rather than a discursive way of knowing, one that is suggestive rather than fully decoded.[12] A principle similar to what Michael Taussig terms the imaginative logic of discovery.[13] In the following pages, some is fiction and some is not, and I do not pinpoint which is what. Some of the fictitious parts of the book were conceived (or imagined) by me, but most are the product of conversations with some of the people who appear in the book, forms of collaborative imagination. Moreover, the different sections jump between points in time and make no mention of specific geographical locations. As such, this is both an anthropological monograph and a piece of experimental ethnographic fiction[14], one that blends ethnographic fieldwork, observations and writings with various literary devices. Using this approach is not because the ethnographic material cannot say enough in and of itself, but because literature, film, imagination and fiction were part and parcel of the field.

"The world is all too easily stuffed with meaning", writes Simon Critchley.[15] From herein, I hope that will not be the case.[16]

OUDENOPHOBIA

Nobody likes nothing.
I certainly wish with all my heart
that it did not exist. But wishing is not enough.
We live in the real world, where nothing does exist.
We cannot just 'disinvent' it.
Stanley Donwood, Slowly Downward – A Collection of Miserable Stories

PIECES OF GLASS

Some years later we meet again. This time it's in an underground bar in the center of the city, popular among various alternative sub-groups at this time. It's located in a partly demolished residential building, occupying what used to be the downstairs apartment. The day before the bar had held a theme night under the title *Forever Alone Party – Love warms you up but Vodka is cheaper.* Soaked-and-dry-again flyers from the event are scattered around the premises. It was Oz who suggested the bar; they've been coming here for some time and currently it's one of the only places they can go to. We sit in a tiny room, in what is likely to have been the bathroom, on pillows strewn out on the floor, gathering around a stump from a tree that serves as a table. Two bottles of vodka are placed on the stump along with some small glasses, an ashtray and a shared pile of cigarette boxes. We sit and drink and smoke for a few hours. Post-punk is playing; people come and go; some sit with us for a while before leaving again; others just look inside and turn around.

At some point after midnight a young man, let's call him Morrie, joins us and sits down next to another young man, Hakuna, who is a friend of Oz. They cuddle up together while the rest of us continue drinking and small talking. After a while Oz kindly but firmly asks Morrie to leave, so that we can have the room to ourselves, which Morrie does. However, 10 minutes later Morrie returns with a bottle of vodka in his hand. He goes straight to Oz, stands in front of him and says: "If you ever tell me to leave again I will smash this bottle into your face". Oz looks at Morrie with a disinterested expression and coldly utters: "Leave". As a consequence, Morrie smashes the unopened bottle into Oz's face, vodka and splinters of glass flying in all directions, and Oz falling to the floor. He quickly gets up, though, and throws himself at Morrie, hitting and kicking him as violently as he can, and, given the small size of the room, he also hits the rest of us. An indistinct amount of time goes by, but after a while we manage to separate Oz and Morrie, Hakuna and Mushu (another friend) escorting Morrie out of the room while Queenie (a friend of Oz and I) assist me in trying to calm down Oz. He sits back on his pillow on the floor, bleeding from several wounds in his face and on his neck. We do our best to remove the pieces of glass that have slid inside his blouse and we note that a piece of glass has gotten stuck in the side of his neck. He pulls it out, leaving an open flesh wound, small but still producing a significant amount of blood. Queenie and I try to convince Hakuna and Mushu, who soon return, as well as the staff in the bar, that they should call an ambulance as Oz is bleeding quite a lot from what we feel is a relatively unfortunate place. They all refuse, however, stating that "it's nothing", or "it doesn't matter".

Even Oz is determined that there is no problem. "It doesn't matter, REALLY. It's nothing", he says whenever a voice of concern is raised. It takes us around 2 hours to convince him to get in a taxi with us and go to a hospital. There's one in a suburb some miles from where we are, but distance doesn't matter and the taxi-driver doesn't care.

As we arrive, Oz is escorted into a doctor's room by some nurses while Queenie and I stay put in the waiting room. It's large and empty and freezing cold. We interchangeably walk around in circles and sit on the benches along the walls. We've promised Oz not to talk to the guard outside, or anyone from the staff. And if they approach us we are to state that what had happened was simply an unfortunate accident, no one else was involved, no need to call the police, nothing had happened. The vending machine is broken.

After a good while Oz comes back out with five stitches in his neck. He rushes us outside and insists that we go to Queenie's apartment and continue drinking, which we do. There's nothing cognac can't fix.

The following evening we're at the bar once more. "It was nothing", Oz says, and touches the stiches on his neck while Hakuna attempts to put the table on fire.

SUNDAY NEUROSIS

I sometimes feel uneasy on Sundays, particularly in the afternoon. It's a sensation that is difficult to describe, but it could perhaps be likened to a vague sense of melancholia; the loss of a weekend that is coming to an end, and another Monday morning looming on the horizon. It's not that I don't like my job or am averse to the notion of working, not at all; it's just that I really liked the weekend. So during some Sunday afternoons I come to experience this peculiar numbness where I'm not able to just enjoy the hours that are in fact still left of the weekend. I know that it's dumb and that it would make much more sense to just shake it off and enjoy the present. But for one reason or another I sometimes don't. The last days of a long holiday can feel like that as well, or the days leading up to a trip abroad, such as going to see Oz, where I'm often going alone and leaving my family behind. On some level I actually often look forward to what is coming; seeing colleagues again when going to work, or landing in another country where I have something to do, and I know that I will be coming back to my family again or that there will be another weekend or holiday in the near future. But most of the time I seem to end up prematurely mourning that which is coming to an end.

Sunday neurosis is a notion thought to have been coined by the neurologist and psychiatrist Viktor Frankl, who used his personal experience of being in a concentration camp to develop theories about the human search for meaning. Sunday neurosis refers to the anxiety that some people may come to experience when the work-week is over; the sense of existential emptiness that may emerge through the realization that this week, also, did not lead anywhere or amount to anything. The sensation may result in a state of boredom, cynicism, or apathy and lead people to question whether their lives have a point or not. Frankl referred to this condition as an "existential vacuum"; a crisis of meaninglessness.[1]

My own uneasy Sunday mood is not completely similar to the sensation described by Frankl, and the background for it obviously very much different, but it is somehow related in terms of the loss of meaning at hand; I have a problem letting go of meaning. It might be an occupational hazard; my line of work consists of conveying meaning to others, of providing understanding through text or through presentations. At least, that's how I've often conceived of it myself. Having read Frankl, and others similarly arguing for the centrality of the notion of meaning, I'd also assumed that this was what people in general strive for, that the search for meaning is a general human condition. Until I met Oz and his friends.

BEWARE, NOTHING!

In Janne Teller's children's novel *Nothing* the young boy Pierre Anthon one day stands up in the middle of class and announces: "Nothing matters. I've known that for a long time. So nothing's worth doing. I just realized that." After this, he leaves the classroom, goes outside, and climbs up into a plum tree. His classmates are stunned by this and almost immediately they collectively come to feel a strong urge to show Pierre Anthon that he should climb down from the plum tree, and to show him that there *is* meaning in life. That it is *something* rather than *nothing* that matters. They therefore decide to pile together a series of items that are particularly meaningful to themselves in order to illustrate what meaning is. They place this pile of meaning in front of the plum tree in order to make Pierre Anthon change his mind. But he doesn't, and ultimately the classmates' struggle for meaning ends in violence among themselves.[2] In literary circles Teller's book is applauded and it is subsequently translated into a number of languages. But it also creates uproars. Several Norwegian schools ban the book. Some French bookstores refuse to sell it. Parents in Germany refuse to allow their children to read it.[3]

Oudenophobia is the fear of nothingness. It is the fear that may suddenly engulf a person when she or he comes to think of death, and the possible void that follows. Or when thinking about the emptiness of outer space; that, on the one hand, before the coming into existence of the universe there was nothing and, on the other, that the universe is continually expanding into what also appears to be nothing. These are dizzying questions: ones having kept many children awake at night, myself as a young boy included. Some of them are touched upon in the story of Pierre Anthon sitting in the plum tree, and oudenophobia is perhaps what led some people and groups to protest against children reading the novel.

In another novel, *The Trial Begins*, the Russian writer and Soviet-dissident Andrei Sinyavsky depicts how the main character, Yury Karlinsky, begins to have trouble falling asleep. The reason for this is that he is tormented by the thought of one day having to die, a thought that enters his mind especially when he is lying on his back. It is not because his life is in any immediate danger and he knows that if he lived his life more carefully, for instance by quitting smoking, he might very well prolong his life by several decades. Yet still, the thought of having to die, of turning into non-existence while the rest of the world goes on in full vitality, is unbearable to him. That there, upon his death, for him will be eternally nothing. He curses the Soviet authorities for having supplanted faith and individual immorality with Communism, and for having thus deprived him from a soothing measure of self-deception. He abruptly sits up in bed and, despite knowing it to be deadly, lights a cigarette. He feels life returning to him upon each drag, "He was smoking, dead men don't smoke".[4]

We know descriptions of Nothing from both literature and mythology. While in Teller and Karlinsky's novels, nothingness and meaninglessness are existential phenomena that the main characters ponder over, there are other varieties in which nothing is more of a physical being. In Michael Ende's classic fantasy novel *The Neverending Story*, the villain is the formless entity called "The Nothing" which spreads through and devours the land.[5] In Scandinavian mythology the creature Nidhug eats away at the roots of the Tree of Life, threatening to turn the world into Nothing. Yet, contrary to these other textual representations, in Teller's novel nothing, nothingness and meaninglessness are not necessarily bad things. It is *the search for meaning itself*, the keen insistence on meaning, the desperate clinging on to *something* that is the root cause of problems. In the midst of violence and existential threat, it is *meaning* standing forth as the problem.

But nothing and nothingness are not just figures of novels and myths. As this book seeks to illustrate, they at times play a very central part in everyday social life, in various guises and incidents, as does meaninglessness. And they do not necessarily do so in a purely negative sense. But why is it that *nothing* has come to be seen as a figure creating fear? What consequences does this fear have on the ways in which we perceive of and analyze the world around us? And what might be lost in the insistence on meaning and the negation of nothingness? It's interesting why so many people fear nothing. But perhaps even more interesting is why some people don't.

GEOGRAPHY IS POINTLESS

Some years later we meet again. This time it's for a longer period than usual. Unfortunately Oz has caught conjunctivitis, "a bad grammatical virus" as he calls it, which prevents us from meeting up the first weekend that I'm around. But we soon find a rhythm.

A few phone-calls back and forth. We agree on meeting at 4 p.m. in front of Oz's work. Mushu is already there waiting when I arrive. Soon after Oz comes out; we kiss on the cheeks and start walking.

Oz sighs. "A friend of ours just died from liver-problems. My boss's son also just died, from leukemia, he was only 11. The dog of one of my other friends just got hit by a car. And this fucking wind in the city is driving me crazy. And then there's my eye infection. And I started having problems with my ear as well. And it's spring!".

We have to go by his doctor where he picks up a prescription for some antibiotics. He immediately tells the doctor that he doesn't intend to take it before after the weekend. "Because you're gonna drink?", she asks and allows him to wait a few days. We jump into a taxi and head to a pharmacy. The pills are expensive; Oz wonders how people who don't have medical insurance get by. He's still working as a translator for a foreign organization, but on a different project now, and who knows for how long. We jump in another taxi and head towards the suburb where he lives. In the small shop by his building we buy vodka, juice and cigarettes. Oz hates this particular shop. One has to go to six different counters to get various kinds of groceries, and it's much more expensive than other shops nearby. But then, he doesn't bother walking to those other shops either. So we buy what we need to buy here, and hate it.

I tell Oz and Mushu about the different aspects of my new project on "nothing". Oz thinks it's a strange project, but he's happy that I came. He hadn't expected us to ever meet again.

He never expects that when people leave the country, that they'll ever come back. He'll consider going to the art exhibition that I'm setting up as part of my project. Maybe. Though probably not.

He talked to Hakuna on the phone earlier. He had mentioned to him how I had been hanging out with Athos from *The Three Musketeers* yesterday. Hakuna had said he thought I was mad. Oz had reminded him that all his friends are. Hakuna himself had called Oz at four in the morning to announce he had just realized something: that geography is pointless, that it can't be used for anything.

GRAVITATION AND STONE-SUCKING

In *Being and Nothingness*, Jean-Paul Sartre establishes that being and non-being cannot be seen independently from each other; they only exist in relation to one another. Hence, there is no such thing as completely nothing, but there is also no such thing as completely something. This is why it's better to speak of "nothingness" rather than nothing. But then, why not also speak of "somethingness" rather than something? Even though the issues at stake here are deep philosophical questions, the baseline is really quite simple: Nothing/something is not an either/or question. Rather, it is at all times a question of both/and. The same may be said about the notion of meaning: The meaningful can only exist because of its relation to what it is not (the meaningless), and vice-versa.

There have been many depictions of how people seek an escape from the meaningless, fighting Nidhug's gnawing on the Tree of Life or running away from The Nothing. Contrary to this, what follows is an engagement with the meaningless, and a depiction of how nothingness and meaninglessness are intertwined, not just with each other but also with their opposites. This is an approach inspired by Samuel Beckett who, in his writings about nothing, worked on a constant deduction of meaning alongside descriptions of indifference towards this meaninglessness. This was, as noted by Mladen Dolar, not an insistence on complete nothingness, but rather a gravitation away from something and towards nothing.[6] In his reading of *Waiting for Godot* and other Beckett novels and plays, Dolar compares the writing style of Beckett to that of James Joyce. While Joyce, he notes, was interested in infinite addition (n+1), Beckett was interested in the exact opposite: subtracting meaning (n−1). "One can easily imagine", Dolar writes, "the two writers reading their proofs, Joyce relentlessly adding new twists, and Beckett constantly crossing out, deleting scenes, paragraphs, pages. For one there is never enough, for the other there is never little enough".[7]

Dolar goes on to insert Beckett into another literary juxtaposition that is worth taking up here, namely differences between Beckett and Jean-Paul Sartre in their respective descriptions of picking up a stone. In Beckett's novel *Molloy*, the protagonist sets up a system for sucking on stones that he finds on a beach. This is a depiction, writes Dolar, that can be seen as a response to the opening scene of Sartre's *Nausea* in which the protagonist equally engages in the activity of picking up stones on a beach. Yet while in *Nausea* only one stone is chosen, in *Molloy* multiple stones are picked up, and whereas Sartre's hero is disgusted by the stone to the point of becoming nauseous, Beckett's hero indulges in his own disgust, putting the stones in his mouth to explore their tastelessness.

Although both authors are thus interested in the question of meaninglessness (n−1), for Sartre the meaningless and its accompanying absurdity is an existential *problem*, whereas for Beckett it is one of *indifference*: "In Sartre the stone has no meaning, its stupid being there and inertia endow the rest of existence with a stone-like quality – the stone petrifies it and turns it into absurdity". In Beckett "all stones taste the same, they are tasteless, indifferent, so why suck one stone rather than the other? Well, the stone is the creature of minimal difference, or the difference of the same, the difference of the indistinct, and it is the 'indifferent difference' that counts, quite literally".[8]

The two tramps in *Waiting for Godot*, Vladimir and Estragon, have been described by John Valentine as being nihilists in Nietzsche's precise sense of the term: "a nihilist is not one who believes in nothing, but one who abandons belief in *this* world in favor of another world that is (according to Nietzsche) idealized, fictitious and the product of the mechanism of *ressentiment*".[9] Dolar comes to a slightly different conclusion in his juxtaposition of Beckett against Joyce and Sartre, one that highlights Beckett's constant deduction of meaning alongside descriptions of indifference towards meaninglessness. In Beckett, nothing is not necessarily something to be feared.

SUPERFICIALITY

If you look for a meaning, you'll miss everything that happens
Andrei Tarkovsky[1]

DATO DIGS A HOLE AND
THEN HE FILLS IT UP AGAIN

I've been here for a few months now, but there is a problem: if the door is locked from the inside, it cannot be opened again. If you lock it from the outside, it's not a problem. You can always lock the door behind you when you leave, but never after coming in. Then you'll be trapped. I call Dato, my landlord. He doesn't understand it either. Something must be wrong with the mechanism of the lock. He brought even bigger glasses this time, so we can *really* look at it.

There's something else Dato hasn't been able to understand. My meaninglessness. He's been thinking a lot about it, he tells me, as we gaze at the lock. He's not been getting it. He still doesn't get the lock, he says, but he thinks he now gets what I'm working on. "Actually, I do something completely meaningless every single day", he says with a smile while working in the lock-mechanism.

We sit down in the kitchen, light our cigarettes while coffee is boiling, and he begins to describe a field located some miles outside of the city. Every weekday Dato goes to this field, he says, and he starts to dig a hole. It takes a good while to do so: the hole is big. And not long after having dug the hole, he begins to fill it up again. And then he goes home.

It's 8 o'clock on a Monday morning some day in the spring. Dato wakes up. He gets out of bed; he eats breakfast with his wife and around 9 a.m. he leaves their house and drives to a field some miles outside of the city. He meets his colleagues there. They talk a bit, have some coffee and then they initiate the day's work. They take out their tools, mainly shovels in different sizes, and they start digging. They know exactly where to dig as they've dug this particular hole many times before. It was not as such their own idea, this digging the hole and filling it up again. They were very happy that they were given the opportunity to the dig the hole, though. Less happy that they had to fill it up again daily. But such were the premises given.

It's Friday afternoon some day in the spring. Dato packs up his tools and prepares to leave a field some miles outside of the capital. He has just finished filling up a hole that he started the day by digging. He and his colleagues are tired. It's been a long week of digging the hole and filling it up, digging the hole and filling it up. Before going home to his wife he stops by my apartment to look at my lock and to let me know that he does something meaningless almost every single day. I ask what the background for this digging and filling up is, and he tells me.

Dato is a professional. Digging is a significant part of his life. He works at the National Museum. He's a recognized archeologist. He's been part of numerous archeological excavations in the country during the last decades. The apartment I rent from Dato is packed with old and new books covering every aspect of the country's history. Dato's good at digging. He has found a significant amount of important artefacts while doing so.

Currently there's a pipeline under construction in the region, carried out by a multinational oil and gas company. Dato is in charge of a series of archeological excavations at selected sites along the planned route, aiming to ensure that no national heritage is lost once the building of the pipeline is initiated. One of these sites is a hillside some miles from the capital. During the excavations, Dato and his team are obliged to adhere to the security regulations of the company, of which one states that due to the potential danger of a car driving into the hole during night-time, trenches are not allowed to be left open. The reason for this is that there is no electricity available at the remote hillside so it's not possible to set up lights so that a car can see the trenches at night; in the darkness a small fence and some signs are deemed not to be enough.

It's true that there is no electricity at the hillside. And it has not been possible to bring a generator because there are no roads. However, given that there are no roads at the hillside there are also not any cars. Dato and his team have to walk there. But still, Dato says, the oil company insists that regulations are kept for the sake of the odd chance that a car will appear at a site where a car cannot possibly go. What this entails is that Dato and the others spend the first part of their day getting to the site and digging their hole, and after lunch they spend the latter part of the day filling it up and walking back.

"Isn't this meaningless?" Dato says to me, and smiles.

It's Sunday morning, and Dato recollects his week.

BLOOD AND GRAVY

I've only just arrived a few days ago and I keep thinking to myself "What kind of splatter is that?" The question roams in my head for days. Had I known a forensic scientist I would probably have called that person to inquire into bloodstain analysis. What was the angle of impact? Are there any points of convergence? Perhaps it's because I have little else to do when I'm in the apartment that I've become so focused on it, that spot on the wall.

Dato's apartment will be rented by someone else for another month, so meanwhile I've found an alternative place to stay on the same street. Although the house I'm in is as close to the city center as one can get, surrounded by ancient landmarks newly renovated and high-modernist hotels newly constructed, it is not in the best of shapes. When observed from the outside, the house looks like it's about to plunge to its own death. It resides, along with numerous other buildings, on the very edge of the steep cliffs overlooking the river running through the city. Most of these buildings have been here for centuries. Still, they look like they are slowly but constantly being pushed towards the edge, ready to crash into the river or into the traffic that rapidly moves along the road that occupies the only strip of land between water and cliffs. The houses look a bit like the coins in the kind of slot-machine where you put in money in the back-end and hope that this will push the pile of money piled up in front to collapse. Money piled into the city center, pushing. And it does happen that a building collapses. Such as half of the building that I am living in now. That could be why the owners no longer live here themselves, and why the rent (considering the location) is relatively low, and why I apparently am the first person to ever rent it. Even the woman from the rental agency seemed slightly disturbed by the place when we met there for me to get the key.

"We have many other apartments in our catalogue", she noted, "in case you change your mind".

At that moment in time I had no intention of going anywhere else. I'd just lost my credit card in the airport (because I forgot it in an ATM); I was tired from travelling; I missed my kids back home and I'd been waiting outside for the rental-lady for almost an hour with a phone that was out of battery. I just wanted to get the keys and get settled. But after having spent 10 minutes alone in the apartment, I knew that I should have said yes to Oz's offer to sleep at his place during the first part of my stay. But then, he was down with the bad grammatical virus.

I find the strange-looking spot in what was supposed to have been my bedroom. Sizewise, it is a significant spot. Just above the bed, covering an area of around one-by-one meter. Of course, it is by no means certain that the spot has been created by blood splatter. The small individual spots are a darkish brown, with a hint of red, and it looks as if they have all landed on the wall with some speed. It *could*, to my untrained eye, be blood. But it could also be gravy. In any case, I choose to sleep in one of the other rooms in the apartment, not least because there is an odd smell and no windows in the spot-bedroom. But I nevertheless return to look at the splatter now and then, prompted by curiosity. It seems that it can't be washed off unless one also washes off part of the flower-patterned wallpaper. I try to dissolve some of it at one point to get a better idea of what it is. I'm being very meticulous about it; I've bought new wash cloths and a type of cleaner that is supposed to be good for walls. While gently rubbing the new cloth on a chosen part of the spot I'm interchangeably telling myself that this is incredibly dumb ("I'm standing in a foreign country investing all my energy and effort into dissolving a spot on a wall, and I'm even writing notes about it") and telling myself that there is something intriguing about the endeavor ("I could ask the neighborhood about it; she doesn't seem to want to talk but perhaps this could be an entry point. Perhaps I could even write a whole story about this house based on the spot!"). I change between being thankful that nobody can see me doing this and wishing that someone was here with me with whom I could share the experience.

The dissolved liquid gives off a distinct smell of bouillon. It has to be gravy. This makes the potential story about the splatter a little less interesting. Yet still, what has happened here that has ended up with somebody tossing a large amount of gravy violently against the bedroom walls? Who's done this? What is the story behind it? I know that I'm not supposed to be asking myself these kinds of questions. That is directly opposed to what I'm supposed to be doing. But so far I can't help but constantly do precisely that.

DUSTING

There are many kinds of digging and many kinds of surfaces. Some are a question of the physical practice of digging and the physical quality of a particular surface, others are merely metaphorical, and others still are a bit of both. In one account on digging, the anthropologist Nadia Seremetakis describes an exhumation practice where women mourners dig up the bones of deceased family members and dust, wash and sun-dry the bones. The dust is removed so that it does not interfere with the sensory relation between the mourner and the deceased; without dusting "they cannot 'see' the bone in the divinatory sense" that is needed in this particular ritual. However, she notes, the dust on the bones is itself not devoid of significance, as it is the dust that encapsulates the material allegory of the temporal chasm that separates the living from the dead. Seremetakis relates the question of "dusting off" the bones to anthropological research practice. In the same way as archeologists dust off bones and pots to "expose" culture, anthropologists "dust off" social structures, kinship, networks or exchange systems in order to get at that which is "behind" such phenomena, what *underlying* meanings one might excavate. But the relation between dust and what it covers, she says, is not a relation of appearance and essence; dust itself can be a subject of analysis just as much as the senses, objects and experiences that dust interrupts and blurs.[2]

Paul Stoller has elaborated on Seremetakis' observation in stating that dusting off as an anthropological endeavor not only clears an object of sedimentation, it also kicks up clouds that obscure our vision and potentially cuts us off from actually engaging in alterity.[3] That is there are potentially types of otherness that disappear from view, not because they cannot be seen but because we overlook them. For instance, when we look for meaning what is it that we don't see?

THE BONES OF FATHER GABRIEL

Not far from the capital, in an ancient city, oil is flowing from a grave in a monastery. Someone will be digging here soon. It won't be Dato; he is busy digging a hole nearby. It was a local nun, Mother Easter, who revealed the occurrence not long ago, just before Orthodox Christmas. She had had a vision that all who were to come to the grave before 7 January, the day of Christmas, would be granted two wishes. Immediately after, hordes of pilgrims, men, women and people with disabilities went to the site. The grave belonged to Father Gabriel, a local monk revered for his piety and who was believed to have possessed the power of healing and prophecy. Allegedly, the monastery earned millions from selling wax candles during these hectic days of pilgrimage. The price of candles had been much higher than usual. The miracles, however, are not for everyone. The church authorities make sure to highlight this.

"The notion that everyone will have all their wishes granted cannot be true, as those requests which are pleasing to God and which are in line with the will of the Lord are fulfilled, not just any desire", states one.[4]

Only the requests of the truly virtuous are granted. However, "Father Gabriel's intercession for the worshippers before the Lord" would continue even after Christmas, another statement assured.[5]

Not long after, the grave was dug open to examine whether a miracle had in fact taken place, whether the bones of Father Gabriel were in fact not even merely bones but actually a complete body that had not decomposed at all. Besides clergy, only members of government were allowed to watch. Afterwards, information about what had actually been found in the grave was contradictive: no conclusive answers were given. But the bones of Father Gabriel went on tour. Although Mother Easter herself eventually denied ever having had a vision (saying she had only asked Father Gabriel to fulfill the wishes of the faithful), the bones are a blockbuster everywhere. Numerous people want to see them or at least be near them. In a suburb in the capital, Oz shrugs his shoulders.

OBSTRUCTION

<imagine here a quote from a Morrissey song>

I HEART GLOOMY

"I'm not really enjoying the fact that you´re here", says Oz, "sorry about that".

He and Hakuna meet with us on the street after having given the taxi driver directions over the phone. It's late in the afternoon and we're going to Giacomo's place, where I haven't been before, nor have I ever met him. We buy vodka on our way there, and walk towards the apartment with arms around each others shoulders. We haven't seen each other for a year or so. I'm actually on my way home, having spent a few weeks on a consultancy job in a north-western region of the country, and I have a few days to spend in the capital before flying out, just enough time to see old friends.

Although I don't know Giacomo, I know about him, as with most of the people who surround the crowd of Oz, Hakuna and Mushu. But I remember having seen pictures of him. They often feature him alongside his motorcycle, and they often feature him shirtless. He looks different from many of the others in the crowd; he's bearded, muscled, tough. Over the next years we'll meet now and then, but not regularly. He's not someone who's always there. He's around somewhere. He comes and goes.

Giacomo lives with his parents, but he has his own, very personalized, section in the apartment. The room we enter is dark and it's centered around a small table surrounded by couches. Some of the bricks on one of the walls have been painted in different colors, otherwise the walls are bare. The main feature of the room, however, is what hides underneath the biggest couch. It conceals a door in the floor under which steep steps lead down into a basement. It's pitch dark as we enter the room below. Giacomo turns on a dim light and, as he does, an almost

21

royal or fairytale-like bed is revealed in the center of the room. "He has a lot of female friends", Oz notes.

We go back up the stairs, drink a bit and play charades. Oz reassures us that we shouldn't be offended by him saying that he's not enjoying our company. "It's more because I'm not enjoying it enough"; he'd like to enjoy it more as he's actually glad we came, only...he just doesn't. He did, however, enjoy reading my book, noting that "I liked it, it was depressing". He didn't really care for my theoretical argument that much, and the fact that I was constantly trying to make sense of things. Given that the world doesn't, why should writings about the world attempt to do so? "You could make it even more depressing if you tried to write about us; you could go global with it", he says. Only, if I was ever to do so I'd have to promise to leave behind my apparent compulsion to make sense. I say that I'm not sure I'd know what a pointless analysis would look like, and if it was to be done it would require us spending a lot of time together, and we might not actually enjoy each other's company.

A few hours go by and little by little the trip to the north-western region is beginning to get to me. I lose track of the conversation and my eyes are eager to close. I also want to enjoy the evening as I'll soon be leaving the country, but like Oz I increasingly don't. The drive to the capital began at 4 a.m. in the morning; we'd taken what was supposed to be a shortcut but ended up getting stuck on a mountain range in the midst of a flock of sheep. When we finally arrived I spent a few hours taking some people to the airport and returning a car after which I had to find a hotel room. It's Easter so everything was booked and it took a few more hours of walking from hotel to hotel before I finally found a room where I could leave my luggage and take a shower before heading to Giacomo's. Now it's past midnight; below me is a secret room with a fairytale-bed; in front of me is a man telling me to stop making sense; next to me is Mushu who rarely says much. I give in to fatigue and doze off; I don't know for how long. As I wake up, Mushu offers to join me in a taxi to the hotel, he's also leaving.

The challenge posed by Oz continues to roam in my head after I leave Giacomo's apartment. Oz's comment annoys me, mainly because I keep thinking that he might be right, that his skepticism towards my writing might be well-founded. I just don't know what to do about it.

EXIT-ENTRY

I walk a bit down the road outside my apartment and hail the first taxi driving by. We settle on a price and go to the airport. I talked to Oz shortly before I left. He's sure that I'll probably never come back.

I get a taxi from the airport. There's a sign just outside the arrival hall stating a fixed price. Ever since the day it was put there taxi drivers have been saying that the price is outdated. I talk to one of the drivers, discuss the price and head towards the city center. We smoke cigarettes together on the highway. He asks me if it's my first time here.

I walk around the corner to get a taxi, but there aren't any passing through my street today. I'm late. There's a new-looking black Mercedes parked on the corner a few blocks away. I knock on the window; he's available; he gives a price three times the usual fare. I curse myself for having gone to find a taxi just next to one of the most expensive hotels in the city; had I given it any thought I would have just gone in the opposite direction, where taxis are always cheaper. I look at my watch and accept the price. I talked to Oz shortly before I left. He's sure that I'll probably never come back.

I get a taxi from the airport. There's a sign just outside the arrival hall stating a fixed price. Ever since the day it was put there, taxi drivers have been saying that the price is outdated. I talk to one of the drivers, discuss the price and head towards the city center. We smoke cigarettes together on the highway. He

23

asks me if it's my first time here.

I walk a few blocks away from the main street. Today I'm not late. There's an old grey Mercedes parked on the corner. I knock on the window; he's available; he gives a price that's below the usual fare. He asks whether I'm in a hurry which I'm not, although of course I have a flight, but we're in good time. "Good", he says, as there's one thing he really needs to do first if that's ok; it'll only take 5 minutes. He turns his head and nods towards the back seat. I realize that there are actually three of us in the car. Behind me a young boy is sitting in complete silence, I hadn't noticed him at all. "My grandson", the driver says, "we need to take him to his kindergarten; my daugther's ill so I promised to do it, 5 minutes". We drive for a good 10 minutes until we reach the grandson's kindergarten. The two of them go inside and the grandfather is back 15 minutes later. "Now, the airport!" he says and sets the car in motion. We drive out of town. Halfway to the airport he turns his head towards me and asks whether I'm in a hurry, which I now slightly am. "Ok", he says, but there's one thing he really needs to do first if that's ok; it'll only take 5 minutes. I ask whether there are other grandchildren hidden in the car. He laughs. No, there isn't, but we're out of gas. I talked to Oz shortly before I left. He's sure that I'll probably never come back.

I get a taxi from the airport. There's a sign just outside the arrival hall stating a fixed price. Ever since the day it was put there taxi drivers have been saying that the price is outdated. I talk to one of the drivers, discuss the price and head towards the city center. We smoke cigarettes together on the highway. "Ah, Modern Talking, my favorite band!", he exclaims as an ABBA song bursts from the speakers. He asks me if it's my first time here.

THE APRAXIA CHALLENGE

One of the antecedents of nihilism is ancient skepticism. It was Gorgias who put forth one of the first known statements on skepticism with his thesis on nothing: "Nothing is; even if something is, it is unknowable; even if it should be comprehended, it cannot be expressed to another".[1] In the later Pyrrhonist school, people such as Sextus Empiricus further argued for a shift from *praxis* to *apraxia*; that is from action to inactivity.

One of the central arguments against skepticism is the so-called Apraxia Challenge (or "inactivity objection"): If a skeptic holds nothing to be true, then she or he is not able to act. Hence, the Apraxia proposed by the Skeptics is variously accused of self-destruction, animal-like behavior, plant-like inactivity, inconsistency, paralysis and the impossibility of living what constitutes a "good" life in the sense of, by virtue of not acting, not being able to choose to perform better rather than worse actions. For Sextus, in his questioning of the rationality of belief, skepticism is in fact exactly this; a skeptic is indeed one who is not acting but it is still someone who is active in the sense of suspending judgment.[2] This position, argues Richard Bett, should be an ethical one; "a skeptic was someone who suspended judgment, and this attitude of suspension of judgment was something one held on to not merely when engaged in theoretical discussion, but also when engaged in the activities of everyday life".[3] One of the benefits of leading a "skeptical life" was the possibility of achieving *ataraxia*; tranquility or freedom of worry as an opposition to dogmatic outlooks.[4] A related notion to apraxia and ataraxia was that of *apatheia*. In its modern usage, the notion of "apathy" is defined as a lack of emotion and denotes indifference. In the original meaning of apatheia, however, absence of passion is also implied but without the same immediate negative connotations. Apatheia was used by the Greek Stoics to convey stability and composure; the Roman Stoics referred to a similar principle, calling it Equanimity.

But the philosophical discussions of apatheia, ataraxia and apraxia came to a sudden end. Manfred Weidhorn writes in *An Anatomy of Skepticism* that "with the rapid spread of monotheism,

25

skepticism abruptly vanishes. The idea of One God and One Truth, as well as One Church to speak for the former and interpret the latter, leaves no room for dissent or doubt". This particularly held true in the Middle Ages. And even in the Renaissance, where Greek thought was increasingly reconsidered, the works of thinkers such as Montaigne and Cervantes were still perceived as "dissenting noises" in a world of venerable belief.[5] Even though there were some who took up the tarrying with the skepticism and nothingness that had once preoccupied people such as Gorgias and Sextus, explicit engagement with such notions was potentially dangerous. For the Church "nothing" was not only an impossibility, but a heresy. As God was eternal, there could not be nothing, and never have been nothing.

One of the casualties of this outlook was the number zero. As Robert Kaplan puts it in his natural history of zero, while it had teased the Greeks and lived a careless life in the East, it came to suffer in the West.[6] Ronald Green, also tracing the history and fate of zero, notes that "fear of the unknown was part and parcel of the theological reason that drove the actions of the Church. A well-ordered universe, the earth at its center, surrounded by the sun and planets; that made sense. But to allow Copernicus and, later, Galileo to disseminate the idea of an infinite universe with an unknown number of worlds...that was unthinkable". Copernicus, and after him also Pascal, were working on theories stating that there were places outside the known universe where there was neither man nor God – there was just nothing, and they knew this to be a dangerous feat. Copernicus therefore hid his findings for most of his life in fear of the consequences of it being known, and Galileo was convicted of grave suspicion of heresy for following Copernicus' position and ended his life in house arrest after having been forced by the Inquisition to denounce his work.

Science kept putting forth new obstructions to the ban on Zero and Nothing, and little by little they made their return. But still, a gap occurred and as a consequence, the question of "why is there being instead of nothing" had, according to Heidegger, not been properly posed since antiquity.[7]

I HEART EUCALYPTUS

In terms of cleaning, window frames are by far the worst. The thick layers of soot emanating from the busy street below requires numerous wipes and changes of water. Two of the windows do not close completely which makes small amounts of soot-heavy air enter constantly. I try to fix the crevices with tiny pieces of toilet paper crumbled together, but it's a futile endeavor. No, wait, actually window frames are not the worst. The fungus on the kitchen walls is the worst. Not least because the most severely affected areas are the ones near the refrigerator and the only available cupboard for storing food. I remove the spots that I can reach and I put all food items in a blocked window by the kitchen entrance (one that does not open out to the street. It doesn't open at all actually). The hallway leading to the toilet is in an equally bad condition. I think of the vast amounts of eucalyptus-cleaner I will use on it each time I pass by. Eucalyptus-attack. I am not as such a fanatic when it comes to cleaning. People who know me will testify to that. Yet I spend hours and days washing soot off panels, walls and window screens, attacking fungus with ever-increasing amounts of eucalyptus. It makes me feel responsible and old, unfit really to study what I do: carelessness, meaninglessness, disengagement. Eucalyptus appears to mean far too much to me for me to actually engage in such things, which makes me hate the soot and the fungus even more.

So why am I staying in this apartment? For one it's prepaid for 2 months, so it wouldn't make sense to leave at this point. Smell, soot and fungus was not mentioned in the ad, and those things aside there is not really anything wrong with the place. It's located on a street in the city center where I've lived before, some 8 years ago. Back then it was in another apartment, one that

I will be moving into again in May, after the 2 pre-paid months in this one. So the neighborhood is familiar. And there are actually things about the apartment that I like. I like the brightly colored pink paint covering the walls in the kitchen (the parts that are not fungus-green). I like that the other part of the building in which the apartment is located is in a state of complete ruin; that from one window I can look directly into what also used to be an apartment, with parts of tiles still on the walls. I like the family of cats in the next-door ruin who serve as my neighbors. I like that I am right above the river, only separated from it by a busy road, and that I can glance endlessly at the murky turquoise water flowing by. I like that I can hear cars roaring by, and the steps and shouts of my neighbors, the car alarms, the police sirens, the city. Perhaps I even like some of the smells because, although not knowing exactly what creates them, they remind me of other places I have lived in this country. It conjures up a strange form of nostalgia, one that mixes present discontent with fond memories.

But then come the moments where I really hate it, where living in this place completely lacks a point. It's here, the point, now and then, but in the midst of fungus often only as a distant memory of a purpose. In such moments all incentive is lost, and the whole thing seems to have been more engaging when it was just an idea that was yet to be realized. A nice and unrealized plan. Now it's just fungus and eucalyptus. And fuck the view over the river. Some sleep would be nice. Have a drink, have a smoke, clean a bit, write some notes and then try to sleep.

After that it sometimes changes once again. Particularly if I leave the house. Then I come to think that what I also like about living in this particular spot is that just down the street there is a certain basement. Steps lead down to it from the outside, although there would be little point in going down right now, as it's currently empty. However, a decade or so ago it housed a bar and restaurant known colloquially as Ameron's. And I used to go there regularly, most often with Queenie. This was where I first met a guy named Victor, who a year later introduced me to a guy named Oz, who is one of the main reasons why I am now here and why all this is being written at all. But I am getting ahead of myself. First thing first: My name is Whiskey.

YES WE CAN'T!

It's Sunday afternoon. Hakuna is still sleeping as I reach Oz's apartment. He asked me to bring some yellow grapefruit juice, some mango juice and a pack of Winston White ("White, NOT light"!). He's walking around with a big glass of beer. His plan for today had been to get a haircut, do some proper shopping and then go somewhere to eat. None of it has or will happen, he says; he's much too tired. He did manage to order pizza, though. Those who had come by last night had actually gone home relatively early. But at some point late into the night Hakuna had called from a discoteque saying that he was coming by. So the two of them had been up til late. Hakuna was already "drugged sleepless" when he arrived. Now, the table is crammed with empty and half-empty packs of cigarettes, juice-glasses, vodka-glasses, ashtrays, plates. We wash juice and vodka glasses for ourselves and leave the rest. Oz puts on Pet Shop Boys and we start emptying one of the leftover vodka bottles. After three glasses, he declares that he's "finally coming to life again, although I don't know whether that's a good thing or a bad thing". The hangover is rough today. "I should just completely stop drinking. Or start drinking constantly, instead of this". He asks me about the art exhibition I'm working on at the moment. "Not that I really care about the content; I'm just wondering whether I know any of the others involved". He doesn't. Pizza arrives, along with some dumplings. "This is the place that's always full of guys, right?", the delivery boy asks. We watch some of the Morrissey documentary again. Oz just finished reading Morrissey's autobiography. "It's well-written, but content-wise not really worthy of being called a classic". He finds some loudspeakers and plays a song from his phone, a Morrissey B-side, Christian Dior wasting his life on grandeur and style.

We melt into the couches and re-watch the scene from Tarkovsky's *Mirror* in which a gust of wind rides across a field of grass. And then we watch it a few more times, freezing the frame now and then. At around 5 p.m. we make a joint attempt to wake up Hakuna. His face is colorless and his eyes distant as he slowly comes to life. He has enough energy to give us a hug, though. Oz tells him to put on some clean socks, he'll let him borrow some. We talk about Morrissey's upcoming tour while Hakuna stares into a wall. "There's a song entitled "Istanbul" on his new album, so he'll definitely go there", says Oz. "I might go there, I don't know. Everyone tells me to, but nobody bothers coming along, and how would I get tickets bought then, and a hotel room booked, and things like that?" Hakuna puts on his pants while trying to give us a headbutt. We go to the living room where Hakuna gulps down some juice before pouring a vodka shot. "Are dumplings kebabs"? he asks and looks befuddled, after which he complains that pineapple juice tastes like cilantro. He doesn't really remember anything from last night, only that he, for fun, had tried to flirt with the taxi driver through the rear-view mirror as they were driving to the suburbs, and that it had nearly caused the car to crash. A new bottle of vodka is opened. Hakuna pours a bit of it on to his plate and attempts to put it on fire. Someone texts Oz to ask whether he wants to have sex. He doesn't, not right now anyway with Hakuna and me present. We empty the bottle. Morrissey sings for us.

NON-LINEARITY

How and why did the line become straight?
Tim Ingold, Lines, A Brief History

ATHOS IN THE PARK

The sun is shining now and the wind has finally subsided. Oz is still ill and I don't have any particular plans today so I decide to go to the park to read. I only brought one book, C.M. Cioran's *A Short History of Decay*. I've been reading fragments of it, but never the book in its entirety. Now seems a good time.

In the park only one bench is not taken; it's lively here today. I go and sit down, and start reading. After having gotten through the first few pages, from "directions to decomposition" to "the faculty of indifference", a man approaches me. I know this is where I got to in the book because I noted down "tattered" on the margin of the page. The man is wearing heavily-worn black clothes and carries a large bag over his right shoulder. He sits down next to me. There's a heavy scent of unwashed cloth and skin surrounding him. His teeth and nails, those of both that are left, are blackened. But amidst this, he has a well-combed and an almost aristocratic black beard and a proud posture. After sitting down, he immediately strikes up a conversation and introduces himself as Athos, from *The Three Musketeers*. "Everything is horrible here", he proclaims after this introduction. "Beautiful, but horrible". He used to live in another capital, he explains, in another country, but no longer, unfortunately. He opens his bag and begins to look around for something. After a good while he pulls out an old briefcase containing vast amounts of plastic pockets. In each of these are one or several drawings, all made by himself, he says. They've been done with pens in various colors: black, blue, green, red. We start looking through them together. The first part are drawings of various historical and mythological figures. Many of them are of Sisyphus rolling his boulder up the hill, or disheartened watching it come back down. A few others are of Alexander the Great, although he stopped portraying Alexander after he learned that he might have been gay. "I don't like that", he says and flips the pages. The second part is portraits of people he's met on his way and the final part a collection of cut-outs from old magazines about the city we're in, from "the Golden Days", 20, 30, 40, 50 years ago. He proceeds to show me his calendar. He doesn't actually use it as a calendar, he notes; it's many years old so that would be pointless. Rather, he uses it to save the names, phone numbers and addresses of people he's met on his way. He asks for mine and I note them down, writing my country of origin instead of my exact address. Upon noticing where I'm from he instantly finds a piece of paper and begins to sketch a group of Vikings on a ship heading to the coasts of England and France. "They'll conquer!", he exclaims and he scribbles away, noting also that he himself has the blood of knights running through his veins.

Before long we're embroiled in battle together, fighting side-by-side. Athos and a random Viking have transcended time in order to campaign together against a common enemy. After we have emerged victoriously from the bloodshed, he puts down the drawing and finds a loaf of bread in his bag for us to share in celebration. We sit and chew side by side, now and then giving each other a nod of acknowledgment. After our grand celebratory meal we shake hands and bid each other farewell. Athos gets up, bows and walks away. I still have a bit of bread left in my hand and notice that it's almost as dirty as Athos's clothes, but I still feel a strong urge to finish it. After all, we won.

SOMETHING DOESN'T HAPPEN
(AND SOMEONE IS NOT THERE)

In mid-May 2014 something does not happen in the capital. An event does not take place. Yet curiously, quite a lot occurs as a consequence of this nothing happening.

That which does not happen is a silent flash mob. The year before, on the same date, the event was violently attacked by an angry mob led by local priests. The police did little if anything to interfere and numerous people were severely injured. This year the event is cancelled. Nevertheless, an anti-demonstration takes to the streets, demonstrating against something that is not there.

I go to see what's going on with two friends, Conchita and Donna, both foreign artists working in the city at the time. We all have gay friends in the city but none of them want to go out. And for good reason. The atmosphere on the main avenue in the city center is tense. A group of anti-demonstrators have gathered in front of the old parliament building where speeches are being given. Speakers are railing against the immoral and meaningless nature of homosexuality. We make our way up front. Facing us is a small boy standing with a sign in his hands. The sign has the word "LGBT" crossed over. Behind the boy, men dressed in black clothes and stern faces stand tall. The boy looks a little confused. Not far away a tent has been put up. Inside people can sign a petition against an anti-discrimination law that was recently passed in parliament. The people gathered are anti anti-discrimination. Donna notices a group of young men who are pointing at us and most likely discussing the fact that we are not there because we are in agreement. We finish our cigarettes and go to my apartment a few blocks away. Cars drive by with young men hanging out of the windows yelling hatefully. The group in front of the old parliament is later joined by another group that has walked from the central cathedral, led by priests. Their steady outbursts resound throughout the city center for the rest of the day.

What was supposed to take place never happened. The event that the anti-demonstration was demonstrating against was not there. Still, hate emanated through the air as sound and tension. This was the only night that the neighbors in my backyard locked the gate to the street. "It's impossible to know what will come of this", said one. The following day someone has placed small pieces of paper on walls and lampposts in the city center. The paper-slips feature a small image of a rainbow and the words "I am here". Somewhere else a collection of shoes has been left on a square signaling the absence of a group who do in fact exist, but who are not allowed any actual presence.

SIDEWAYS

As Tim Ingold has noted, the straight line has in many ways become an icon of modernity as something that offers reason, certainty, authority and a sense of direction. Yet, as he goes on to argue, "too often in the twentieth century, reason has been shown to work in profoundly irrational ways, certainties have bred fractious conflict, authority has been revealed as the mask of intolerance and oppression, and directions have been confounded in a maze of dead ends".[1] In this sense, he continues, while the straight line has been an icon of modernity, the broken or fragmented line has emerged as an icon of postmodernity.

But still, even though fragmentation and disorientation may be seen as exemplars of postmodernity, this does not seem to entail that ideas of the straight line have become obsolete. On the contrary, there are many aspects in which the straight line continues to dominate. As Sara Ahmed shows in *Queer Phenomenology*, daily life for many people is still very much a question of following straight lines, being directed along them and being in line with others, with the effect that the body gets directed in some ways more than others. "The lines that direct us", she writes, "as lines of thought as well as lines of motion, are in this way performative: they depend on the repetition of norms and conventions, of routes and paths taken, but they are also created as an effect of this repetition".[2] As a consequence we become committed to what lines lead us toward and where they take us, and to us taking note of and relating to that which is "of course" rather than to that which is "off course". In other words we become oriented, and through repetition risk getting stuck in particular forms of alignment. This may entail a bodily aspect (in terms of bodies being shaped by certain repetitive tasks), but also aspects of perception and thinking in the sense that we stop noticing the regularity we are in and the fact that we may have begun to act and think along particular straight lines. Consider the following scene where Ahmed and her female partner enter the dining room of a holiday resort:

> In front of me, on the tables, couples are seated. Table after table, couple after couple, taking the same form: one man sitting by one woman around a "round table", facing each other "over" the table. Of course, I "know" this image – it is a familiar one, after all. But I am shocked by the sheer force of the regularity of that which is familiar: how each table presents the same form of sociality as the form of the heterosexual couple. How is it possible, with all that is possible, that the same form is repeated again and again? How does the openness of the future get closed down into so little in the present?[3]

WINDS AND MIRRORS

One afternoon, after having spent the night at Oz's place, and the morning in his kitchen eating soup and drinking beer, and mid-day not taking a walk, he asked which Tarkovsky films I liked. Which was none, as I had never seen any. After what I remember to be a very long silence, he suggested that we start with *Mirror*. Filmed in Russia in the early 1970s, *Mirror* is Andrei Tarkovsky's seventh film as director, and it is often seen as a cinematic expression of the stream of consciousness principle most often found in literature, although in a more fragmented manner than in the latter. Not long after the film had started, Oz froze the frame. The wind-scene was coming up and this I should take note of (mentally, that is, not on paper). And so we watched it. And then he played back, and we watched it again. And then he played back. The scene is difficult to describe. I tried many times as Oz sent me a link so that I could re-watch it in my apartment ("there is a man walking across a field and as he is midway a gust of wind suddenly appears out of nowhere, creating waves in the long grass. The man stops. And then it happens again; the wind blows through the grass. And then the film continues"). But others have managed in a more succinct manner, one of them Thomas Redwood who details it as follows:

In shot VII of Scene 1, after the first gust of wind ripples through the field past the doctor, the spectator is presented with a close-up image of Masha standing in front of a row of trees and looking to the left of the frame towards the doctor. After a moment's reflection, Masha then turns to the right of the frame and begins walking to the dacha (...) The next shot (IX) cuts back to a long-shot of the doctor still standing in the field as another strong gust of wind passes through (...) This is followed by another close-up of Masha (shot X) back where she was at the beginning of shot VIII, in front of the trees, once again staring toward the left of the frame(...) Masha then, once again, moves rightwards towards the dacha and at this time the camera follows her. In other words, just as the two shots of the doctor presents a repetition (of the gust of wind) so do the two shots of Masha. Shots VII and X have shown her performing exactly the same action. Viewed attentively, the structure of this brief early sequence clearly negates any sense of straightforward spatial and temporal logic (...) Rather than functioning to represent a linear sequence of events (a sequential continuum of time over four successive shots), Tarkovsky's strategy here serves two explicitly non-linear functions. Firstly (...) the two shots of the doctor in the field establish the wind as a significant motific device. Secondly (...) the two shots of Masha cue the spectator to infer that decoupage sequences in Mirror cannot be relied upon to present transparent linear arrangements of diegetic space and time.[4]

Let us dwell for a moment on the notion of "decoupage" mentioned by Redwood, before we return to Oz's apartment. In French cinema, this is a term that describes the last stage of scriptwriting as well as a film's structure after the final cut has been made in the editing room. It may, according to Valerie Orpen, be translated into "continuity editing"; a conceptualization of film "as a convergence of the spatial fragments of the shooting process with the temporal fragments established in editing".[5] It thus differs from the notion of montage, most often associated with Sergei Eisenstein, which is a way of cutting something into sequence and solely a mode of editing. Tarkovsky himself was strongly opposed to Eisenstein and the use of montage in film, as he saw montage as a question of fragmenting reality and then reorganizing it into a dialectical framework from which new ideas and new meanings were meant to emerge. Tarkovsky's method (for instance in his use of long takes) was instead one of shifting focus from narrative to duration and thus creating a semantic crisis where "the meaning is not imposed on the viewer, but is always hidden away or scattered in time. The constant expectation that semantic implications will reveal themselves in the single continuum of the long take tends to exhaust the viewer. No quick-and-easy resolution is available; hence Tarkovsky's notoriety as a challenging or even 'boring' director".[6]

Tarkovsky insisted on editing not to be a formative element of a film; a film is not made on the editing table, as montage cinematographers held. Instead, while finishing *Mirror*, editing "was a serious test of how good our shooting had been".[7] He was critical towards montage cinema's belief that bringing two concepts together engendered a third, new one. As he notes, "'Montage Cinema' presents the audience with puzzles and riddles, makes them decipher symbols, take pleasure in allegories, appealing all the time to their intellectual experience. Each of these riddles, however, has its own exact, word for word solution". Tarkovsky instead sought to work towards a narrative technique that was deliberately puzzling to the audience and if asked what his film "meant" he replied that they "meant nothing other than what they were".[8]

Based on the principle of non-linear decoupage, Tarkovsky's alternative to narrativity, linearity and montage was to conceive of film as a question of what he termed "sculpting in time". Nariman Skakov writes in relation to this conception that the term "cinematography" is inherently spatial in that it consists of the terms *graphia* (writing) and *kinema* (movement) and becomes a principle of inscribing motion. By referring to his own practice as a question of sculpting in time, Tarkovsky conceived of a process that still retains the question of inscription (through sculpting) but replaces *kinema* with *chronos*. The objective becomes one of capturing temporal flows. It is significant here, Skakov mentions, that the word Tarkovsky uses for "sculpting" is the Russian verb *vaiat* which is also related to the notion of "weaving". This entails that his films "have a certain texture, a textile labyrinth, where the relationship between individual temporal threads (past-present-future) is not immediately apparent". So again a question of non-linearity and scattered time. The long takes and the often complete absence of action creates a certain monotony in Tarkovsky's films; there are rarely (if ever) any high points. There are no events that stand out as more significant than others. There are long passages where nothing takes place; a principle by which Tarkovsky shares an affinity with Samuel Beckett. And Tarkovsky was in no way interested in clarity. Indeed, in his diaries he describes how one of the reasons behind the break between himself and Vadim Yussov, the cinematographer he had worked with on *The Steamroller and the Violin, Ivan's Childhood,*

Andrei Rublov and *Solaris,* was that Yussov "worked only with certainties...That's bad".[9]

Mirror is a classic example of the principle of sculpting in time in that it consists of a series of frameworks that remain un-unified via an overarching narrative line, which makes any narrative reading of the film impossible. There is no differentiation between past, present and future, and no clear explanations of what is dream, memory or reality. Tarkovsky wanted to create a reflection without necessarily revealing what was reflected.

THE ROAD TO NOWHERE

It's easy to get lost when trying to reach Nowhere. Most times I do; the streets in this part of town all look the same: Faded facades abrupted now and then by newly-painted ones, cigarette vendors, mobile phone shops, out-of-order ATMs. The first thing to remember is to turn right at the Marriott Hotel. After that you have to turn left which is when the tricky parts begin, especially if you're trying to reach Nowhere at night, which is most often the case. The streets all look the same and unless you remember the street name (which I never do) you'll have to turn left on all of them until you stumble upon the right one. And this is when it gets even more tricky, because there is no sign saying that you've reached Nowhere. The only direction you get is that it's located in the basement of a now-closed foreign cafe. Large parts of the cafe's interior are still in place: the counter, some chairs, a few tables, a refrigerator. Along with these are small piles of rubbish scattered around the floor and in the ceiling a fluorescent lamp is flickering. A handful of people are hanging out in the room, standing by the walls, talking silently. But this itself is not Nowhere. Nowhere is downstairs. And there is not a sign directing you there.

DETOURS

"Would you tell me, please, which way I ought to go from here?"
"That depends a good deal on where you want to get to", said the Cat.
"I don't much care where', said Alice.
"Then it doesn't matter which way you go", said the Cat.
Lewis Caroll, Alice's Adventures in Wonderland

HAKUNA'S GONE FISHING

He does that from time to time, goes missing without a trace. It worries Oz. It also annoys him immensely. The last thing he heard from Hakuna was that he was planning to go to the Sunday flea market, which apparently he did and people say that they saw him there. But since Sunday evening nobody's heard anything from him. He doesn't pick up his phone, which is unusual. And he deleted his Facebook account, which is less unusual. "He doesn't smoke weed at the moment", Oz says. "But maybe he's at a police-station again, or perhaps he got into another fight somewhere". He pauses for a moment. "You know, he's actually a really sweet guy when he's sober". We call him now and then during the day and evening but there continues to be no reply. We also call his girlfriend to ask her whether she's heard anything from him. She hasn't. She asks us whether she should be nervous. Oz tells her not to worry, "he probably just packed his tent and went fishing somewhere".

A holiday is coming up. Oz plans to spend it much the same way as he spends his time at work, watching *Buffy the Vampire Slayer*, reading *Harry Potter* and playing Throne Wars. But he needs to set up a drinking schedule so that he doesn't end up drinking every day. Perhaps he'll just reverse a normal week; instead of staying sober on weekdays and drinking throughout the weekend, he'll drink during weekdays and stay sober at the weekend. We should go to his family's summer house in the countryside, he says. It's not much, but it's peaceful in the garden. If Giacomo comes along we'll have a car; Mushu could come to, as could Hakuna, if he's resurfaced by then. With a car we could stack up on everything we'd need and then spend a few days, or even a week, in complete isolation. We talk about the things we could do while there. We never go.

SUSPENSIONS OF BELIEF

It's been years since I last saw Sahara. The last time we met was, I think, back when we went together to Victor's mother's summerhouse. We'd jumped on a train from the capital and jumped off again once the train reached the middle of nowhere. We walked to the cottage, swam in the river, drank home-brew, sang and laughed late into the night, slept a few hours and then went back.

Sahara and I recently connected online and at some point after that I wrote to her because I remember us once talking about atheism. I'd been thinking about maybe doing a project about atheism, something on suspensions of belief or suspensions of meaning, but I hadn't really found an angle on it yet so needed to talk to someone in order to get some initial ideas about where and how to start.

Sahara responded by writing that "everyone I know here is either an atheist or a nihilist. You know many of them too". And she was completely right, I realized, and wondered why I had never thought of that; Victor's friends, the ones I had watched Greenaway with that evening, the sighs and cigarettes and Morrissey songs. They suspended more or less everything as far as I recalled, so why not just start with them?

Alternatively one could of course also start with Søren Kierkegaard. In his philosophical work *Fear and Trembling* ("*Frygt og Bæven*"), Kierkegaard retells the biblical story of Abraham who, childless at the age of 80, prays to God for his wife to give him a son. After being granted the wish, Abraham's wife Sarah gives birth to Isaac. Yet as Isaac reaches the age of 30, God orders

Abraham to kill him. Abraham prepares for the sacrifice but at the very last moment, God tells Abraham to spare Isaac and kill a ram instead. Kierkegaard retells the story in four fictional versions and uses these to consider the relation between religion and the ethical, claiming that although the killing of one's own son is ethically wrong, it is, in the story of Abraham, religiously right, which is what paves way for Abraham's anxiety. Abraham was aware of his ethical wrongdoing but his faith in God told him that the latter would, in the end, spare his son. Kierkegaard takes this to be a case of "teleological suspension of the ethical" in that Abraham puts his ethical concerns in the background; although killing his own son is an unethical decision this knowledge is suspended in favor of the *telos* of God's righteousness. For Kierkegaard, Abraham only agrees to kill his own son because he has *enough* faith. This is what allows him to suspend the ethical. Had he not had enough faith, he would not have agreed to kill his own son in the first place.

Sextus would most likely not have agreed. Nor would that crowd of people watching Greenaway, even though they suspended all the time. But doing a project based on them and their perspectives would necessitate something of a suspension on my behalf as well, a more or less clean break with most of what I had been doing research on and writing about up until then. But also offer a chance to, if not kill a ram, then at least go astray for a while. Wander a bit in the dark.

THE ADVENTURES OF MOBY

...and at some point he realized that he had been walking for hours, thinking about Moby. So now he had no idea where he was. In some kind of suburb probably, but it could be anywhere in the city. Concrete high-rises, swarms of cars, the sun going down. He found himself standing in front of an old football field, slipping in and out of registration of his surroundings and his thoughts about Moby. He had begun to have some concerns about her, or rather their, business venture, about what it would lead to. And then there were the more personal feelings, about what their relation might or might not lead to. In the middle of the football field there was a small wooden shed. Its location was odd, there, right in the middle, obstructing the possibility of using the field for anything requiring someone to run straight across it. He kept staring at it. Moby. Shed. Moby. Shed. Moby. Shed. Moby. Moby. Moby. Shed. At first he had thought it was empty, but after several minutes he realized that there was someone inside. Probably three people, the disappearing light made it hard to tell. Yes, it was three. Young boys. He wondered where Moby might be at this very moment, what she was doing. Who she was with. On the lookout for possible buyers most likely, but where and who was impossible to say. The three boys were up to something, one standing in front of the other two. Was he pulling his pants down? Moby could also be at home, or with Doc Doc or the Priestess, or both of them. They were all supposed to meet later that evening and discuss their plans; he was inevitably going to be late, by right now not knowing where he was. Yes, one of the boys, the smallest of the three, was definitely pulling his pants down. The other two just standing still, looking. He would have to figure out where he was so he could begin to make his way to the meeting, there was much to talk about and he looked forward to seeing Moby. The small one pulled his pants up and they all left. So did Gregor Samsa.

...but what would be the best way to start a business in this country be? They had been discussing it for ages, over and over and over again. Perhaps setting up a production of backs for chairs so that there would be something other than stools. Or perhaps something involving fixing toilets or making soft pillows? Or maybe produce and distribute cocaine? Yes, cocaine; there's a market for that. More than for chairs.

...and so it was settled. And the idea to start the operation below a church seemed almost too perfect. Who would ever suspect such an endeavor operating from within such a place? Gregor Samsa would grow a beard in order to look like an orthodox priest and thus uphold an outwards appearance that made the place dis-appear and not dys-appear. Meanwhile, Doc Doc and Moby would take care of production and dealing; Doc Doc had the knowledge and Moby had the contacts. Finding a vacated church, however, proved tricky; all churches were all in use and there was not enough start-up funds to build a new one from scratch, not even a cheap Protestant version. After some deliberation and a few phone calls back and forth, the team instead moved in with The High Priestess.

... and now they were all meeting there, only Gregor Samsa didn't know where he was. As he looked again the field was empty. Maybe no one was ever there.

AN INHUMAN GATHERING

In late 2015 an artist posts a statement online concerning an attack that had recently taken place in the capital against *Campus Studio*. This was a space where students, artists and architects had been meeting for a series of different events, including artist talks and discussions of a range of various theoretical texts and perspectives. The statement read as follows:

Since many of the lectures drew between 100 and 150 people, Campus Studio used loudspeakers, so that the audience could hear the lecture on the street and in the yard. During one of the lectures Nietzsche's quotation 'God is dead' could be heard on the streets. This apparently caused some of the neighbors to believe Campus Studio to be a meeting space for satanic gatherings, luring young adults and children. On November 15 three young adults from the neighborhood interrupted a lecture and one attacked co-founder and director with a knife. With serious lung injuries and blood loss, he survived after an extensive operation and days in intensive care. All this happened, once again, in the name of faith and religion. Not only has the Church fueled hatred and ignorance, but the government has been looking away over the past when crimes in the name of religion have been committed, ridiculing the secular aim manifested in the country's constitution.[1]

The "once-again" in the text refers to a series of violent attacks having taken place in the country in recent years against individuals or groups condemned by the Church. Some of these were carried out by fanatic followers, some were officially condoned by the Church, and some were carried out by priests themselves. For local clergy, nihilist tendencies have long been seen as a highly problematic phenomena coinciding with other "subcultures" not fitting into the worldview of the Church, and believed to cause a serious moral problem for the country and its population. This stems from the perspective that believing in *something* lies at the very basis of what constitutes a human being; not believing, whether as an atheist or a nihilist, inevitably renders a person "un-human" and devoid of morality.[2] Yet the people who gathered in and around Campus Studio during the event that caused the attack were not necessarily either atheists or nihilists, they were simply discussing Nietszche as they had been discussing many other theorists.

But it was not just clergy who feared nihilism. Several local politicians had also been depicting it as a major societal disease. Particularly young people, they held, were increasingly disengaging from social, religious and political life. Nihilism was a malaise, a wart, a dys-appearance on the surface of a land that fully made sense.

HIJACKED

I've met Cleo a few times before, at her own apartment. From what I remember she's equally obsessed with her parrot, cooking mushroom dishes and dancing. We've danced a lot whenever meeting, and we've eaten a lot of mushrooms. She also brought a small dish to Oz's place this evening, and she insists that we all eat and dance. She even manages to convince Oz to dance, although he's only on the floor for some 5 seconds to show a short bit of a Michael Jackson dance routine that he spent days and weeks perfecting when he was a teenager. Despite its brevity, he leaves the small audience stunned.

Oz knows Cleo through her son, who is one of his old friends. They stopped being in touch completely, but he still sees Cleo now and then. Usually they meet at her apartment, but tonight she came here. Cleo's husband, David, is also with us this evening. We talk a bit about my work and at some point I mention atheism. "If you don't believe in God then we can never talk together again", he exclaims. Then he laughs and Cleo gives me a firm kiss.

Past midnight I decide it's time to go home. Cleo and David suggest that we share a taxi as their apartment is on the way to mine. We say goodbye to the rest of the company and with Cleo leading the way we dance down the stairs and along the street where we hail a taxi. Once arriving at their apartment, Cleo insists that I come up for just one drink, despite my insistence that I really just want to continue in the taxi towards my own place in order to sleep. But there's nothing to do. We take the elevator up and Cleo immediately puts on music and starts cooking. We have mushrooms and a few drinks and say hello to the parrot after which I say that now I really have to go, which prompts Cleo to go to the bedroom. She returns shortly after with sheets and a pillow, and while David tries to prevent me from putting on my jacket, Cleo converts the sofa into a bed. It takes ages, repeated hugs and multiple kisses and a few more drinks before I make it out the door. Once again in a taxi I receive a text from Oz who asks whether I made it home. Upon my reply that I have he writes that he's surprised that I ever managed to get out of there.

It's difficult to just disappear. Saying no is virtually impossible.

REPRESENTATION

"In the old days", he said, "writers' lives were more interesting
than their writing.
Nowadays neither the lives or the writing is interesting".
Charles Bukowski, Pulp

DIY PET CREMATION

The printing house is closed during Easter; we all forgot to think
about that! This'll be a problem in terms of getting the texts for
the exhibition catalogue printed in time. Alternatively people
can get the cover at the opening and then they could return
at some point later to pick up the content. That's not an ideal
solution at all. But in any case the covers have to be cut and
folded Thursday, and we need to buy the string to sew together
covers and contents (if the latter ever gets printed). Friday and
Saturday we will put up the wallpaper in the gallery and buy
paint for the window frames. Paint Sunday. Dry Monday. Install
works Tuesday and Wednesday. We still need a video projector.
And despite the best of plans there is always the risk of getting
stuck in traffic somewhere, or being met by a stickler in a shop;
petty annoyances and project-ending occurrences.

We take a break and listen to some music. Seated on stools in
Conchita's kitchen we discuss the Black Bloc, distorted alphabets,
why Cobra art doesn't work and Ulrik's old project about pet
cremation. He's discarded his original idea for the exhibition
and decided to go for something else instead, something about
leather jackets and chandelier crystals. Possibly crystals inside
the jacket. We'll need to go to the market to scout for materials.
The others are still sticking to their original ideas; the metro,
commodities, solitary sounds, ruined landscapes. With all the
loose ends in terms of preparing the gallery, at least some things
are coming to a close. We discuss what a possible playlist for
the after-party might consist of. The party will be held in the

basement below the gallery. Wine has been arranged. Ulrik asks us what our lazer sounds are. The great thing about the Beach Boys' *Kokomo* is that it's about a place that doesn't exist. We found a pink fluorescent lamp at the market; it *has* to be part of the exhibition somehow. We'll need to think about that. If you listen carefully, this is art. Cheap sheeps. Present to me a seven-titted animal. Sales at the pharmacy. Olivia can't find the eggs she needs for her installation and the wallpaper is coming down in the gallery; we probably haven't used enough glue; this is a disaster. Conchita kicks out another artist, the ruin-piece; now we're down to four, and we still keep stepping in the paint. Lightbox, spray paint, wall plugs, wine for the reception, print the letters or cut them in glittery paper? We desperately need a screwdriver.

"What's that?" one elderly man says to another as they pass the gallery. "It's nothing", says the other. So, at least in some sense, we're ready.

PIT-STOP ON THE CONE-TRAIL

It was somewhat by chance that I met Conchita. We had known about each other for some years as we had mutual friends. One of them was Queenie and she had continuously suggested that the two of us should meet if we were ever in the same city at the same time. We were, Queenie had said, the kind of people who would either get along immediately or instantly dislike each other.

In the spring, some years ago, I flew in as I had to do a consultancy job in the north-western region of the country. Queenie, who was coming along, arranged for us to stay overnight in Conchita's place in the capital before heading north. Despite Queenie's worries, Conchita and I got along immediately. She had lived in the country for some 5 years at this point. Herself an artist, she was working at the local center for contemporary art during that period and had a short-lived background in anthropology. For some time I had pondered over mixing anthropology and art in my own work (without much success), and besides some work-related commonalities we shared a deepfelt love for books, cognac, cigarettes and conversation. We talked about various literature at length, about what made writing good, and how more academic texts ought to be like that. Good, that is. It ended up a long night, first in a restaurant, afterwards in her kitchen.

Some 6 months later I received a grant to conduct research about nothingness and meaninglessness. Although I had a relatively clear idea about what to do in terms of carrying out the data collection, I had been grappling with the question of how my eventual data could ever be turned into text. I began looking into how this might have been done in other disciplines, exploring questions such as how nothing for instance could be transformed into an object in an art gallery. These strains of thought had led me to think about Conchita and although we hadn't really been in touch since our brief meeting earlier that year, I wrote her an e-mail asking whether she would be interested in setting up some kind of collaboration about this issue while I was conducting fieldwork. How would she approach the question of representation as an artist? If it had, for instance, been a question of setting up an art exhibition where nothingness was to be given a physical form, what would she do? I also asked her whether she would be interested in doing exactly that with me during my upcoming fieldwork. Her immediate response was a definite no. She had, just a week prior to receiving my e-mail, promised herself to never curate an exhibition ever again. But then, after some consideration, she said yes anyway, and that's when our troubles began.

Our first realization was that our project was not as such novel. Not at all, in fact. Just as with its prominence in literary fiction, Nothing has been a theme in the artworld for some time, and a long series of artists have created works based on the notion, from when the visual zero emerged as a component in relation to the vanishing point to when the group "Les Incohérents" created a series of one-colored fabrics as a cynical remark on abstract art, including *First Communion of Anemic White Girls in Snowy Weather* (1883), *A Harvest of Tomatoes on the Edge of the Red Sea Harvested by Apoplectic Cardinals* (1884) and *Total Eclipse of the Sun in Darkest Africa* (1889).[1] And many more works from many more artists appeared since then, some as a parody on art itself and others seeking to make a point about the notion of nothingness, such as Yves Klein's exhibition "Le Vide" (The Void), opening in Paris in 1958, consisting of an empty gallery and later considered to be one of the first examples of conceptual art (or at least the first to gain wide publicity). And particularly since the 1950s and 1960s, whether through minimalism, avant garde, installation or pop art, artists have sought to tangle and conceptualize Nothing. John Cage's 1952 composition 4´33″, a performance where a pianist sits at his piano for 4 minutes and 33 seconds without doing anything, after which he takes a bow and leaves; Robert Barry's *Closed Gallery* (1969), consisting of a locked gallery in Amsterdam with a note on the door stating "for the exhibition the gallery will be closed", and Ad Rheinhardt's *Black Pictures* series which consisted of repetitions of the exact same black square painting; a series he started in 1960 and repeated for 5 years in an attempt to represent art as "breathless, timeless, styleless, lifeless, deathless, endless".[2]

Pondering over these antecedents, Conchita and I have long, rambling conversations about how to approach the setting up of an exhibition, who to contact or invite, where to do it and how to prepare, and whether to do it at all.

STREAMS

When William James originally coined the term "streams of consciousness" in 1890 it was to depict consciousness as something which is not joined but flowing.[3] As a narrative device to portray inner dialogue, it has since been used extensively in literature, from Virginia Woolf and William Faulkner to Samuel Beckett and Hubert Selby Jr. For the latter, most notably in *Last Exit to Brooklyn*, it is not merely a question of the inner dialogue of an individual, but equally of dialogue between individuals gliding together in a stream. The text refuses to present the reader with any "she said" or "he yelled", but instead allows one to overhear a conversation, discussion or argument through words passing by.

In discussing the interrelation between literature and ethnography, Gabriele Shwab draws on the work of Hans-Jorg Rheinberger in defining literature as an experimental system that has the potential to "generate emergent forms of subjectivity, culture and life in processes of dialogical exchange with its readers".[4] For Rheinberger, experimental systems are "spaces of emergence that invent structures in order to grasp what cannot yet be thought", what he also terms a question of playing in the dark. Fumbling your way through thoughts, bumping your head into unforeseen obstacles, moving around them, going elsewhere with no clear fix-point in mind. One might draw a parallel from this to the Theater of the Absurd, and the works of dramatists such as Arthur Adamov, Samuel Beckett, Jean Genet, Eugene Ionesco and Harold Pinter. Martin Esslin, who can be credited with defining the term (or movement), notes how many of the people who may be said to have been part of creating the style of the Theater of the Absurd were in various ways inspired by dramatists such as Salacrou, Sartre and Camus who had been writing about the anguished, senseless and absurd conditions of human existence. Yet they differ from these, writes Esslin, in that the mentioned dramatists had presented "their sense of the irrationality of the human condition in the form of highly lucid and logically constructed reasoning, while the Theater of the Absurd strives to express its sense of the senselessness of the human condition and the inadequacy of the rational approach by the open abandonment of rational devices and discursive thought".[5] An antecedent to this dramaturgic approach was Bertolt Brecht who had argued for a change in theater entailing a break with the traditional method of seeking to create a psychological link between a character on stage and the audience. The latter had involved a principle of trying to make the audience see or feel the world from the point of view of the actor.

The problem with this, for Brecht, was that if an audience simply adopted the point of view of a character they would not be able to think critically about what was going on. Hence, a certain alienation effect had to be present in theater.[6] Eugene Ionesco later held that Brecht did actually not take this principle far enough and that theater had to employ shock tactics in order to truly overthrow and dislocate the spectators' perception of reality.[7] The motives and actions of those on stage had to remain incomprehensible. And similarly, returning again to the question of literature, Gabriele Shwab notes that "texts that appear unfamiliar and strange force one to deal with their otherness and foreignness".[8] The effect of this being that a particular work does not close something down (or conclude) but rather forces the reader to open something up.[9] The strength of a text is not necessarily to reveal but rather to afford an opportunity to think.

In *Walter Benjamin's Grave*, Michael Taussig cites the following passage from William Burrough's "The Literary Techniques of Lady Sutton-Smith": "Cut-ups? But of course. I have been a cut-up for years...I think of words as being alive like animals. They don't like to be kept in pages. Cut the pages and let the words out".[10]

What I truly love about my own copy of *Walter Benjamin's Grave*, which was bought second-hand, is that the previous owner has torn out around one-third of the "Authors Notes" and "Chapter 1", leaving them almost in themselves as cut-ups, and leaving me playing in the dark in order to grasp what the arguments of those sections might be, or could be, as something is literally missing. On most pages I have absolutely no idea what Taussig is trying to tell me, and that's what keeps returning me to the text, to the words still left.

WALLPAPER FRENZY

I wake up to find that Oz has deleted me on Facebook.

I'm at Conchita's place around noon. We have coffee in her kitchen surrounded by books, print-outs and notes. She made a sketch for the sign to hang outside the gallery. It needs to be done in a material that can survive being outdoors as heavy rains might still occur, but also one that it is possible to cut into, some sort of plastic probably. She's in the process of making measurements of the gallery to calculate the potential amount of wallpaper that will be needed, plus the amount needed for publication covers. If rolls are roughly 50cm wide we will need around 24 rolls in total. We've both been commenting on Leo's text during the last couple of days. I like the idea of using Spivak's notion of sub-alterns to discuss the sub-urbs. So does Conchita, but she worries that he'll been offended by our criticism and suggestions. We have more coffee, eat a banana, talk a bit about her renovation plans for the apartment and her considerations about leaving the country for good. We have yet another final cigarette and head out to find a minibus that will take us to the central market. Conchita's been there quite a few times before, so have I, but never to the wallpaper section.

"It's like heaven and hell", she says as we move through the endless rows of small paths and alleys, "you can find everything here, but it's impossible to know exactly where and how long it will take". We roam around at random for a while before asking a shop-owner for directions. Shortly after we locate the "wall-paper street". Dozens of small shops lie side-by-side, all crammed with wallpaper in all shapes, colors and sizes. Our vantage point is to find a pattern with small flowers but all we see are grand flower patterns wherever we go. After half an hour or so we reach the end of the street. We have a cigarette and buy some meat and mashed potatoes from a vendor. We need to look through all the shops once more, even more meticulously this time around. And finally, in what seems to be the messiest of all the shops, we find two types that we sort of like, and which would fit well together. One has small yellow, beige and green flowers, the other is a sharp yellow with rows of yellowish spots. We ask the owner how many rolls he has of each and he disappears into a mountain of wallpaper rolls in search of the two types. One by one he throws them down to us and we collect them in two piles. It takes a good while and a lot of rolls end up in the piles. But there are not enough of either one.

Conchita remembers seeing the sharply yellow version in one of the other shops, so we buy the ten rolls available where we are and go to the other shop, where we buy two more. At that place we also find a large flower patterned version in white and glitter. It doesn't completely fit with the other, but we agree that in a way that in itself fits the principle. We also agree that we forgot to think about how to transport 24 rolls of wallpaper back to Conchita's apartment.

CONSCIOUS SEDATION

i'm getting annoyed. now my left ear's plugged or smth. how r u doing? unplug it! i'm good, have just met athos from the three musketeers. will go by the doctor tomorrow before we start drinking. i'm sure we can cure you if the doctor can't. where did u meet which athos? in the park close to where i live. 9 april park. yeah i know where that is. the skatepark? and who's athos? i mean what kind of athos? one of the musketeers. he had a great costume. yes but i mean this specific athos, who is he? have no idea, i think he was russian, now alcoholic/insane/athos. i see. btw the old russian movie 3 musketeers is the best i have seen. i didn't know there was a russian version, lets watch it some time. gladly but i doubt we can get it with subtitles. not that u won't know the story. we can. i think i'll be able to follow the plot. yeah, very likely. otherwise i'll bring athos

to be honest i'm starting to feel too miserable to be glad about anything, but still. how r u?. have a terrible hangover, drank cognac with the artist-group until 6 this morning. i see. yeah i didn't go to my office today either. are you still ill? yes. it's dawning on me. what i did. i don't even know what happened to the paintings. i threw them on the stairs hopefully Hakuna took them. what?! oh you don't know anything about our fight? no. sorry. ok. what happened? can't right now. sorry. no worries, hope you are ok. physically fine. sorry to hear. yeah me too

was calling you i think. at about 6 and just now. yes, i heard it at six but didn't want to get up. and i didnt hear it now. yeah i didn't sleep all night. i mean. really? i went to sleep after that and woke up at 11 or smth. there were things after you left. can't type. will ya come over?. i thought u said something about noon today yesterday. yes, i think i did. i have to spend a few hours packing i think. did you get in another fight with Hakuna? almost. kicked him out twice. tato left on the street. cant type once again. left on the street? what does that mean. will you come over after packing?. toldya can't type. i have to be at the gallery around 16/17, will let you know when i'm done packing (need to go out and buy some stuff). ok. chances of seeing you today are obviously slim. but anyway it was fun yesterday and all ended well. Hakuna is on his way from gldai already. hehe, you always get in a fight after i leave. (where he stayed at Byron's cause i kicked him out, etc.). will be glad to see you if you manage. yeah u always miss all the fun. yeahh. naaa it wasn't really a fight. just a long process of kicking him out and him coming back again. anyway he doesn't really remember anything and all's well. he seemed a bit stoned already when i came. all is perfect in my state of denmark. i think it as just absinthe. was. didn't see any weed last night. not that i looked for it. well, absinth alone can do the trick i think. that he/she/it can, especially 3 of them

havent you gone to bed yet? no. well done. ccant atalk rigjht now\. lol. can even attatck. am unesleep unhaired. haha, ok. and tpoo durnk. and almosyt als[pee.nyway.talk yto ya tomorrow. am pissed aoj tyop of that. aggresivebut non able to spell. unable probably. androwhatever. go to sleep. it's daylight. it's all Hakunas fault. anyway. hes asleep in my room and im beng stupid heer. anyway. sorry. no worries. will call you tomorrowe. today i mean. yes, do that. okm hope ai w9ill go to sleep. jesus. no I won't its already dayu,igjht but at some point I will. anuway. judging from your spelling i think you will able to. will call you when i wake upo hopefull;

INDECISION

Bunny Lebowski: Blow on them.
The Dude: You want me to blow on your toes?
Bunny Lebowski: I can't blow that far.
The Dude: Are you sure he won't mind?
Bunny Lebowski: Uli doesn't care about anything. He's a nihilist.
The Dude: Ah, that must be exhausting.
Joel and Ethan Cohen, The Big Lebowski

HAKUNA WAKES UP

One night, after an uneasy dream, Hakuna woke up and found that he had been transformed into a person with a political opinion.

It is a late August afternoon and I'm walking around with Oz and Hakuna, trying to find a place to hang out. They've recently been banned from their regular cafe, an ad-hoc bar based in a partly demolished building in the city center, so we need to go somewhere, anywhere, else. Oz and Hakuna had been getting into too many fights lately, either with each other or with other guests, and the staff had grown tired of it. On this day in August we've been walking around for a good while. It's late in the afternoon and the heat is excruciating. We've had a few beers in a park, calling some people to find out whether they have a place where we can stay during the evening. Oz detests the idea of going to a regular bar or cafe; they all have some idiotic decor, he sighs; pastiches of either "local traditional style", with their brick walls, wooden furniture and polyphonic singing on the stereo, or "some retro-Buddha-art shit". New cafes and bars have been popping up like mushrooms in recent years, mainly in the newly renovated parts of the city's Old Town district which, in Oz's view, now looks more like a set from a Disney movie than a place where people live.

Hakuna calls a guy he recently met, BQ, and we are invited

to come to his place. BQ's apartment is located in the northern-most part of the old-town neighborhood, but still a place no politician has yet thought of renovating at this time. "A bad neighborhood", Oz notes while we are climbing the steep stairs to reach the door. Hakuna has stopped somewhere behind us to talk to a dog. "A lot of crime here", says Oz, "and people who are crazy. But then, most of my own friends are as well". He tells the story of how one time, while Hakuna was walking down one of the central avenues in the city center, a random guy had yelled "gay" at him, maybe because of the way he dresses, and Hakuna had taken out a knife and cut him, not killing him, Oz says, but still causing some injury. "He likes to cut in stuff, but you already know that", he concludes. Hakuna catches up with us and says that he keeps forgetting my name, can he just call me Whiskey? That will be easier to remember.

As we reach our destination, a pair of drowsy eyes partly covered by wild and messy hair appear from behind the door. BQ lets us in. He lives here with his sister, who joins us once in a while during the evening, and a small black dog. The apartment is largely empty, with small run-down rooms. There is a couch, a few chairs and a small table in the living room, but no other furniture. A few pages from a Swedish magazine have been taped to one of the walls. I ask BQ why they have hung them there. "Not really for any reason", he says. None of them can read what it says. BQ finds an assortment of small glasses in different shapes and colors and Oz takes out the vodka, soda and grape juice that we bought before coming. Cigarette packs are thrown on the table along with an ashtray and someone puts on music. The heat is still stifling and we slowly melt into our chairs, drinking without toasting, listening to music, smoking and chatting. All windows are open but there is no wind and cigarette smoke hangs still in the air.

At some late hour of the night Hakuna and I begin discussing politics. Parliamentary elections are coming up. The current president stands to lose to a relatively new political party. I didn't know much about the new party's political standpoints but I knew the current government, and had been writing about the drawbacks of their grand political visions and how these were implemented. Hakuna says that he is going to vote for the current president. I ask him why and a minor discussion starts. Hakuna notes that the current president has "already filled his pockets", and if a new president and political party comes to power "it would not change anything anyway, just as the last change of power didn´t". Although the political scene changes, politics is as stale as the air of the room we are sitting in. There are differences but they do not make a difference. I do not think much of it; everyone discusses politics in this country, even though no one ever finds politics worth discussing[1], so it seems harmless. Hakuna gets a bit agitated at one point but the conversation soon drifts into something else. My participation ends a few hours later, not because of that particular discussion but because I, like everyone else, am getting drunk and tired. Oz wants to be sure that I make it home safely, and he has a feeling, he confides to me by dragging me slightly aside, that Hakuna will soon punch someone. Probably Oz himself or BQ; they always got into fights, but I should go home before it happens. So I leave.

I don't see Hakuna again for almost a year. The first thing Hakuna did when we met again was to apologize. I had no idea why. "For the discussion about politics we had last time we saw each other", he said. I confided that although I remembered it I had not given it much thought. Still, Hakuna said, he was sorry about it. He had not meant to make a point about anything; I should not take it as him actually having a stance towards, or caring about, politics; he had just been drunk. And so we went along the street to find a place to buy a bottle we could empty. I remember thinking that this was probably the closest Hakuna and I had ever come to having a conversation about something that related to the socio-political context we were in. Surely, it was a conversation that negated the importance of this context, but still. I also thought that perhaps we now knew each other well enough for him to randomly punch me later that evening, as he did his other friends. But it was Hakuna; would it matter?

THE LATTER-DAY DUDE

At this point you might be thinking: "Weren't there a group of nihilists in *The Big Lebowski*?" Which indeed there were, one of them stating to the main character in a heavy German accent "we are nihilists, we believe in nothing".[2] Or, you might come to think of the philosophy of Sartre or Heidegger, or the writings of Dostoevsky, or the story of how people flocked to the Louvre in 1913 after the Mona Lisa had been stolen to see the spot where the famous painting had once hung, but where there was now nothing; among those going being Franz Kafka and his friend Max Brod.[3] Or you might come to think of the TV show *Seinfeld*. In the episode "The Pitch", Jerry Seinfeld and George Costanza sit at their local coffee shop and discuss the possibility of creating a TV show, and based on their own conversation George suggests that they pitch a show about nothing, exclaiming to Jerry who "says you gotta have a story!" and following it up "with everybody's doing *something*, we'll do *nothing*".[4]

This is of course a valid point; that nothing, and the related notion of meaninglessness, exists in many different places and contexts. But there is also an important aspect to take note of here. Namely that just as all the things we can count as being "something" are obviously different from each other in a myriad of different ways (they are something but not the same thing), then all the things we can count as being "nothing" are also different from each other. Hence, there is "nothing" to be found in Sartre, Heidegger, Dostoevsky, *The Big Lebowski*, *Seinfeld* as well as in a random suburb in a random part of the world, but that does not entail that these are the same kinds of nothing. For instance, the nihilists in *The Big Lebowski* represent the principle of creating nothing through destruction and thus share an affinity with the violent Nihilist Movement in 1860s Russia. But this kind of programmatic search for (or use of) nothing is not at stake everywhere. And although Seinfeld is depicted as "a show about nothing", each episode is still built around a distinct plot in which different minutiae of daily life are put into play, and where the main characters are caught up in details that are perhaps pointless for everyone else around them, but which they themselves cling to. Paradoxes and laughs erupt in *Seinfeld* because of people finding importance in something that *others* (and we as viewers) regard as nothing. This becomes clear in the final episode in which Jerry, George, Elaine and Kramer are imprisoned for their "callous indifference and utter disregard for everything that is good and decent"[5]; society blames them for an indifference that they themselves do not acknowledge. But indifference may very well be acknowledged.

OZ GOES OUT

We both wake up around noon these days. We chat a bit online, and sometimes we call each other after chatting. Today is Sunday. I have no specific plans but have considered going to the flea market. To my surprise, Oz has thought the same. He's meeting up with Hakuna, Tatu and Mushu there and will call me when he leaves his house. A few hours later we are in the park. Hakuna immediately disappears into the crowd, chatting and kissing people on his way. Oz and I slowly enter, soon meeting a group of his old friends, all of them surprised to see him there. We step over a small stall where Gillian is hanging out with her daughter and some friends. Oz also knows this crowd. We stay with them for a while before deciding to find Hakuna. I suggest that we buy a drink from one of the punch-places. Oz doesn't want to; perhaps we can get something somewhere else later. He doesn't like the fact that there are so many people here, so we mainly walk around at the outskirts of the market, Oz meeting people he knows everywhere on our way. We circle around for a while, chat with people, smoke cigarettes. Mushu shows up and we go back to where Gillian is. It starts raining and a number of customers and stand-owners begin to leave. We're waiting for Tatu to show up. I haven't seen him for a few weeks, not since we pretended to be Italians one evening at Oz's, who thought it was stupid. We stroll around a bit longer before the group decides to go to Oz's to drink. I decide not to go; we talk about meeting up on Tuesday, which is a holiday.

Come Tuesday we both wake up late and chat a bit. Oz writes that he's going to take a non-drinking day. He still needs to watch the last 10 minutes of the new Robocop movie; other than that "he's going to do nothing". I suggest that we could meet up somewhere. I'd planned to go to the cafe around the corner from my apartment for lunch; he could join me if he wants. He doesn't. Maybe some other time, but today he really wants to do nothing. He's going to the city center tomorrow to take care of some practical stuff; we can get in touch then and perhaps do something.

We meet the next day around 11 and find a small cafe with air conditioning to have lunch. I ask about Gillian and Stephen; are they still separated? A friend told Oz that it was probably something Gillian had been thinking about for a while, as she had been looking for another apartment. They've been together for over 10 years, since their daughter was born. Stephen used to work two jobs, but he quit one of them some time ago and started drinking more than usual after that. That might have been what caused the break. Oz's known Gillian since she was 15 or 16 and he was in his mid-20s. Mushu, her brother, must have been around seven at that time. He lost contact with Gillian at some point, but years later when he and Mushu became friends, they were reacquainted. Mushu is jogging at the moment, but he'd like to meet up with us later. Byron and Hakuna both have dentist appointments and Tatu is at work, but they'll probably all come to Oz's place in the afternoon. He asks me if I feel like having a drink. I could drink a cold beer, I say. He's in the mood for cold vodka. He has some at home, so we jump in a taxi and buy beer and cigarettes on the way.

We're drenched in sweat as we arrive. Oz changes from pants to shorts and puts on Pet Shop Boys. In the apartment it's much cooler than outside, but we're still sweating. We discuss books. He had a year abroad with his parents as a teenager, and he spent the entire time reading. Everything from Stephen King to Faulkner. At present he's reading Iris Murdoch, "she's good, she doesn't write like a woman, thankfully". We disappear into a world of literature for some hours, with Pet Shop Boys continuing their songs in the background, later superseded by Tom Waits, then back to Pet Shop Boys. We talk about Cortazar's *Hopscotch*, and him writing about himself, his friends and what they drink. Soon after, Byron and Tatu arrive. They pour vodka and take off their shirts; Oz finds a fan and we continue talking. Tatu goes down to the shop for more vodka, juice and cigarettes. Mushu arrives. Depeche Mode, Terence Trent D'Arby, Duran Duran. Discussions about chest hair and tattoos. Byron leaves at five; I leave at six; Hakuna never shows up.

WHISKEY STARTS WRITING

I present an early draft of a piece about meaninglessness at conference. Later there's a dinner and afterwards drinks. I'm talking to some old acquaintances in the garden outside the conference venue when two PhD students come up to us. "We don't agree with you at all", one says. The other one takes over and explains how all I said was wrong and basically undermined what we were all supposed to do; describe the meaningful life worlds of individuals and groups. In one sense I want to engage in whatever fruitful discussion we might have, but also I had wine during dinner and I'm enjoying talking to my old friends about something that is not anthropology, so I don't really bother. But I can tell from the posture of the two that really I ought to. Particularly one of them seems both disturbed and angry. "Is this just for fun?", she says. No, I answer, it really isn't.

The following week I have another presentation where I talk about meaninglessness and nothingness. It's with a slightly different crowd. My son is in zero-grade at this point and they have a theme where the children's parents are invited to come and talk about their work. Last week it was a policeman. My son, his two sisters, my wife and I had just been abroad for a month in relation to another research project I'd been doing, and the plan was that we were to show some pictures from this trip. But we soon ended up talking about nothing. It was my son who brought it up because "nothing", as he said to his classmates, "is what my dad is working on". And then we started talking about why that was, how one could work on "nothing", and what "nothing" really was. For me, it was the probably the most inspiring occasion of presenting my work that I can remember. Not because of what I myself said. But because of the way the people present engaged in the subject. We talked about places where nothing exists, like outer space. And what it means when people say "it's nothing", or "it doesn't matter". Like when you're at a playground and one of your friends accidentally pushes you and makes you fall down. It might hurt; you might get a bruise, but you might still say "it's ok; it doesn't matter". Even if it's someone you don't know, that might be your response. But why? What makes things matter? And what makes things *not* matter?

Later, his younger sister asks me if we could write a story about doing nothing. We go to my home office and open my computer. She sits down next to me and asks me to start typing:

i don't wanna do anything

bear doesn't wanna do anything

we're bored

bear dresses up as a dolphin

bear loves to look at the sun

bear loves to look at stars and the moon

bear is still bored

She asks if this is also how I write about nothing, and I say that it probably ought to be; that I had begun writing a monograph about nothing but recently realized that I had been writing it in conformity with how a classical monograph is written; an introduction, a few chapters about the context, some empirical-come-analytical chapters, and then a solid conclusion, and that this really didn't work at all. She starts staring out of the window and we agree that one day we might finish the story. But for now we will leave bear with his boredom, and ourselves do something else.

DOES DIFFERENCE MAKE A DIFFERENCE?

In a recent paper Sarah Green has traced the epistemological logics of geographical borders and the rules for establishing a difference between a "here" and a "there". Based on the case of two uninhabited Aegean islands and the dispute between Greece and Turkey about which country these islands belong to, Green notes that "there are different ways of making sense of the meaning of the 'here' as opposed to 'elsewhere', and these methods often coexist in the same space. This simple condition (the coexistence of different border regimes, each of which uses a different logic to establish the meaning of places) inevitably makes grey zones, ambiguities and uncertainties at the interface between border regimes".[6] What is at stake here is two different places coexisting within the same uninhabited geographical space. Under normal circumstances, this difference does not make a difference; the islands are more or less just a gathering of rocks in the sea that no one really pays attention to. But at one point a Turkish cargo ship ran aground on one of them and the captain subsequently refused the assistance of a Greek coastguard because the island, in the captain's perspective, was Turkish territory and it should therefore be the Turkish coastguard coming to his assistance. Now, suddenly, the difference began to make a difference.

In her account, Green outlines a paradox of border-making; a situation where the drawing of borders, which is usually perceived as an act of creating clarity, ends up creating anything but clarity. In other words, rather than removing the ambiguity of what is here and what is there, differences within epistemological logics underlying the making of borders may end up as grey zones where "heres" and "theres" begin to intermingle or overlap. The overall question, then, is when does a difference begin to make a difference?[7] Or we might pose the similar, yet opposite, question: when does difference continue not to make a difference?

FREEDOM

Where there is purpose you will always be in misery
Osho, The Empty Boat

WELCOME TO THE ANTI-CHURCH OF HATRED

There are two churches as you enter the building, located side-by-side on the third floor. Make sure to ring the door bell to the left, and not the one to the right. The latter will take you to what some would characterize as an "ordinary church". One from which joyous toasts can occasionally be heard; celebrations of the glorious nation we are in, the firm identity of its people, its age-old cultural values, its strong religious bonds, collectively performing a quest for certainty. This is not the church that we are visiting today, although it generally seems to be the more popular of the two. But we will go left today and we will make sure to watch our steps in doing so.

Some initial directions are in order. A good thing to know before going there is that taxi-drivers will not necessarily know where this address is, as we are no longer on the left bank of the city center, and who would want to live on the wrong side of the river? And a few notes before we ring the door bell: You will discover a sticker shaped as a cross next to the door we are supposed to enter. This might cause some confusion as this is in no way intentional. Indeed, the high-priestess has, to the severe discontent of her neighbor, elaborously tried to remove it, scratching and peeling, but so far with no luck. It's a stubborn marker.

She is likely to be busy inside. The interior of the church is under continuous renovation. Or at least there are plans to renovate everything. In May probably. Or June. Or later, who knows? It could feature blue tiles in the bathroom (they are expensive, but wouldn't it just look great? Perhaps it should just be done and then screw the expenses!). It's ok to bring up the theme of renovations during a conversation, as long as you don't sound as if you're rushing her. She doesn't respond well to that, she doesn't like to be rushed, she takes the time she needs. This goes for everything from renovating the church to rolling her cigarettes. The imported tobacco is a treasure, and alongside the equally imported coffee among the most sacred items in the church.

I make it sound so easy. But rest assured, she will make you leave if you don't perform your very best.

When she goes out among other people her opinions and exclamations are not always appreciated, not even when she is being ironic. Some people are, for instance, offended when she says that she doesn't really like children. But maybe that's because they don't get that this is as much about not liking the way children are perceived and handled in general, or that adults are simply more interesting to carry a conversation with. Don't you just hate people who get offended so easily? They try not to show, but their mouths do in the way they tighten the minute such an utterance is heard in a restaurant. Loosen up will you; stop being so pretentious (go make a useless and uninteresting sculpture somewhere instead; we know you can, go for it!).

There is no consecrated wine in the church, but there is cognac. Blunt worship against worship. Intolerance against intolerance. Possibilities of learning something profound that you'll have forgotten in the morning

DEFAULT MODE

Let's pause for a minute and catch our breaths with a bit of neuro-science. In Ernst Bloch's philosophical account of hope, he depicts daydreaming as a faculty of youth, one that escapes the mind and lives of adults.[1] Indeed, it is almost the burden of every new generation to be seen as day-dreaming or idle youth by their elders, despite the fact that these elders were themselves also seen as such by their elders, and hated it.[2] Consider the principle of staring out of a window. I remember doing it endlessly as a child, and tellingly, while I barely remember what my primary-school classroom looked like inside, I clearly remember the windows: big square ones with frames that were painted in a dark-brown color. And I remember hating being disrupted when staring out of them.

But perhaps doing just that, staring out of windows, is not such a bad idea, neither for children, youths or adults. The neuroscientists Mary Helen Immordino-Yang, Joanna A. Christodoulou and Vanessa Singh have shown how "emerging conceptions of brain functioning reveal that neural networks responsible for maintaining and focusing attention into the environment appear to toggle with a so-called default mode (DM) of brain function that is spontaneously induced during rest, daydreaming and other non-attentive but awake mental states". They refer to studies that have shown how "people with stronger DM connectivity at rest score higher on measures of cognitive abilities, such as divergent thinking, reading comprehension, and memory".[3] "Inadequate opportunity for children to play and adolescents to quietly reflect and to daydream", they continue, "may have negative consequences, both for social-emotional well-being and for the ability to attend well to tasks".[4] I never should have stopped staring out of windows.

But it's not always easy to spot when someone is idle or daydreaming. In interviewing the owner of a website promoting "idle-theory", Tom Lutz is told how "the fisherman (...) may look like he's idle as he sits, intent on his line, but at that moment he is constrained, not free. When he isn't fishing he may go for a walk and look more active, but he is actually free to do anything at that moment".[5]

ET TU BROD?

As Andrushka Gornipotok fell asleep one night he found himself visited by a young jewish man in an uneasy dream. Much to his surprise, he realized that the young man was Franz Kafka. "He failed me", Kafka said to Andrushka. "It was supposed to have been destroyed, absent". Andrushka woke up tormented by guilt. Not his own guilt, but that of Max Brod, the man who had promised his friend Kafka to destroy his work upon the latter's death. For weeks, Andrushka lay sleepless, knowing that he had read something that was never to have been published, that he unknowingly had become an accomplice in betrayal. But then, an illumination: "It is up to me to finish what Max Brod couldn't!". And so he began. He went to every book store and bought every copy, most on credit; there were so many. He burned them at home, and the money saved on firewood (it's freezing outside) was used to buy even more books. He went to every publishing house, under a false name, to let them know that no further books would need to be printed. He went to every library and borrowed every Kafka book. Once home he crossed over every word in every book borrowed and then he returned them to the libraries. He visited all his friends, borrowed their books, crossed over every word, returned them.

Time passed. People went to their book shelves and found something to read. Nobody picked up a Kafka book and even the few who did only managed to get so far as arranging it as an intention on their nightstand. This was good, he thought, but still potentially dangerous. At some point someone would be too awake or too pretentious or too curious and actually pick up the book and start reading. He would have to start over, visit all libraries and all homes once more, only this time with a different motive. This time he had to remove not only the content but also blur the name or the book itself so that no one would ever realize they even had a book by Kafka. And so he returned to all books, altered "Kafka" by adding dots and lines to individual letters in the word, making it unintelligible, on each book differently. And it worked. Soon after Kafka, and the notion of a work by Kafka, had been erased not only in the books themselves but also in the minds of those who owned them.

He went home. At ease, finally. Opened a bottle of vodka and drank, speedily. There was now only one Kafka book left, one he had kept himself. He would spend tonight altering not only Kafka's name but also every single word in the book. Make the Latin script look Cyrillic perhaps. Turn form into nonsense, something into nothing. But the suddenly there was a loud knock on the door. Andrushka panicked. He was so close to the goal. He downed the remaining vodka from the bottle and fell to the bathroom floor, knocking over the toilet on his way down. Vomit and water everywhere, soaking the pages spread around him. "There's nothing to do but eat", he said aloud to himself. And so he did. He gulped down the dissolving paper, chewing faster and faster with each new knock on the door. Outside the windows, everything was beginning to grow light. Then, without his consent, his head sank to the floor, and from his nostrils streamed the ink of Kafka's last words.

THE DOING OF NOTHING

As Tom Lutz has shown in the context of US cultural history, there have been numerous expressions of "doing nothing" throughout the twentieth century; every period has had its own version: idlers, loungers, romantics, loafers, bohemians, saunterers, flappers, beats, nonconformists, delinquents, slackers.[6] There has, to paraphrase Julian Jason Haladyn, been a certain will to boredom present during various parts of recent history.[7] Similar examples of such a condition are plentiful in literary or semibiographical accounts of boredom, inertia and disengagement in modern life, from Robert Musil's *The Man without Qualities* to Fyodor Dostoevsky's *The Brothers Karamazov* and Jack Kerouac's *On the Road*. Boredom, in these perspectives, is a question of nothing happening in the sense not only of no events taking place, but just as much of events taking place that are regarded as nothing.[8] Or, put differently, boredom is not necessarily a struggle with disrupted intentions or desires, but can equally stand forth as an acceptance of the meaningless.

But what does it mean to do nothing? As Billy Ehn and Ovar Lofgren have noted, "redefining some activities as 'doing nothing' could in the nineteenth century be used as accusations of laziness and inertia directed toward common people, and at the other end of the social scale as accusations of indolence among the idle rich". Being bored was thus a question of inactivity that either related to having no possibilities of doing anything, or of having enough possibilities to not care about doing anything.[9] This, according to Ehn and Lofgren, has led notions of domination and marginalization to "slip in through the back door" as means to depict the situation of people who do nothing.[10] Within the social sciences, this has most often taken the shape of analyses that highlight the structural inequalities that render it impossible for individuals to act, that in various ways rob them of their agency. This has been (and still is) a valuable perspective unfolded in various ways, for instance, within practice theory and post-colonial theory.[11] Yet, as Deborah Durham has argued, it is to a large extent Western ideas of the active subject that have configured boredom as something that must be a problem. She traces this to the *bildungsroman* from the eighteenth and nineteenth centuries, and the context of industrialization, in which the personal growth of young people was linked to social change. "As the young person finds a personal agency," she writes, "individuality, the ability to choose among options and to exercise an imagination, he also becomes the agent of social change".[12] Social scientists, not least anthropologists and sociologists, have, according to Durham, clung to the notion of agency as an act of liberation, "restoring to those who seem powerless their individual rights to act effectively upon the world".[13] Or, said differently, they have sought to show that boredom and the doing of nothing is not the fault of the individual but rather, to paraphrase Paul

Farmer, a form of structural violence.[14] Durham furthermore highlights how traces of the Birmingham School, where youth agency was seen as resistance and rebellion through cultural consumption or new identity markers such as dress and music, remains inherent to contemporary understandings of youth, agency and marginality.[15] The problem Durham raises is that this accentuation of (suppressed) agency comes to overshadow instances in which people do not really care what is going on.

What might go amiss in maintaining this focus on youth agency is that questions of deliberate disengagement cannot easily be accounted for analytically. A leading figure in the study of the relation between agency and structure has been Pierre Bourdieu, particularly in his work *Pascalian Meditations*, in which he unfolds the relation between the notions of "illusio" and "lusiones", individual hopes and the probabilities of their actualization. Ghassan Hage has recently noted how his personal ethnographic language has become permeated by Bourdieuvian concepts over the years, not least those related to illusion: "investment, directionality and intensity", and habitus, "capacity, disposition, and habit".[16] These concepts are central in Bourdieu's understanding of social life as a struggle to accumulate social agency within a society consisting of productions and distributions of social being.[17] Hage relates this to the phenomena of eavesdropping and his own personal experience of losing his ability to hear. Hearing, he writes, is not always a purposeful act, and this simple observation contradicts a central aspect of Bourdieu's conceptual framework: "Bourdieu's subject is...an 'oriented' subject who derives meaningfulness from having a purpose in life, or to put it differently, a subject that encounters the world purposefully".[18] Thus, if you do not have a purpose, then you are deprived of being, and this will result in a loss of reality. As Hage goes on to argue, "being" is here reduced to *purposeful* being, and even though Bourdieu sees realities as multiple, there are aspects of reality he cannot account for, as they don't fit into a modern ontology of purposefulness.[19] In a similar vein, Alessandro Duranti has noted that social scientists must reconcile with the fact that not all societies or groups have recognized intentionality as a central frame of explanation.[20]

INACTIVITY, AGAIN

It is perhaps worthwhile here to return to the interrelations between apraxia and praxis, or inactivity and activity, that were prominent in discussions among the ancient skeptics. As previously noted, it was praxis rather than apraxia that came to dominate later philosophical discussions in the West. An example of this would be the work of Hannah Arendt and her focus on *vita activa*, which, for her, designates the basic conditions of life: labor, work and action. Out of these, action (praxis) is the activity most closely related to the phenomena of natality: new beginning. Natality, she writes, "makes itself felt in the world only because the newcomer possesses the capacity of beginning something anew; that is of acting. In this sense of initiative, an element of action, and therefore of natality, is inherent in all human activities." She further notes that human lives are conditioned by more than the basic conditions under which they were given life, as everything they come in contact with immediately turns into a condition of their existence: "The world in which the *vita activa* spends itself consists of things produced by human activities; but the things that owe their existence exclusively to men nevertheless constantly condition their human makers".[21] In short, we are born under conditions and ourselves create further conditions of our existence. Hence, we are always conditioned and we are always active, or at least strive to be.

Arendt draws these conclusions from Aristotle's definition of praxis (action) and lexis (speech) and the political philosophy of Augustine. "To act", she notes, "in its most general sense, means to take an initiative, to begin (as the Greek word *archaic*, 'to begin', 'to lead' and eventually 'to rule' indicates), to set something in motion".[22] This does not, however, mean that all acts are possible. On the contrary, because life is intersubjectively constituted, and because of the conditioned nature of being, action does not necessarily achieve its purpose, "almost never", in fact.[23] Yet, although praxis or action does not necessarily ensure freedom, it is *through or within praxis* and its relation to nativity that freedom has a potential: "The fact that man is capable of action means that the unexpected can be expected from him, that he is able to perform what is infinitely improbable"; through praxis, it becomes possible for people to tell their own stories, thereby gaining at least a sense of freedom.[24] There are clear resemblances between Arendt's focus on praxis and that of Bourdieu; it is the purposeful that potentially leads to freedom. With praxis, in such perspectives, being a central feature of what all people essentially strive toward, it is not surprising that praxis is also what we tend to look for when engaging in a study of social life. Yet, looking back at the ancient skeptics, the purposeless and the inactive may equally be seen as a position of freedom.

DOLPHINS FOR M-

"Their performances were exclusive. So exclusive that they ever only performed publicly once. And this singular event itself was so exclusive that the only ones present were themselves. This is the story of Dolphins for M-."

The group formed in 2014 through a chance encounter. They were an international constellation and despite their differences they were soon to find a common artistic ground that would eventually lead them to places that no-one (themselves included) could ever have predicted. Even at the peak of their collaboration their repertoire remained highly selective. It was built up around a single inspiration, a legendary Dzengiz Khan song from 1980. They would rehearse endlessly by candlelight in various kitchens and living rooms, and in the dusk on terrasses by the coast, surrounded by lemon trees, in anticipation of their once-in-a-lifetime performance.

Shortly after their coastal performance the group dismantled. It has been rumoured that the break-up was a result of internal arguments about who did and did not look chubby on a series of promotional photos. Officially they are taking a break, and while some of the members have been seen together at various times and places, all four are yet to reunite.

We take a morning train and arrive at the coast late in the afternoon. It's strangely odd to be back. It's only been some 5 years since I was last here, but everything has changed. The city looks completely different, with the new high-rises with carrousels on the roof-top and dolphin sculptures by the shore. We've rented a small place to stay further down the coast, in a village a few miles out of the city. I stayed here for some days during the war because it was close to the border and therefore easy to make a quick get away. I'm a little more at ease this time around. After unpacking we take a bus to the city center one night to have dinner. It's in a new restaurant, located close to my old apartment. After we've finished our meal, some local artists who know Conchita drop by and I drop out, going to my old backyard. It looks the same. Long lines of laundry intermingle above; children are playing football in the yard, and above there is my old balcony. But amidst all the sameness, something is missing: all the people I once knew here are gone, some have migrated, some are in prison, some have passed away. I spent months here once, trying to make sense of things. With everyone now gone, I wonder if I ever really managed to. Or whether I tried too hard.

WONDERLAND

<verse 1>
allt sem engin et sal at
sem to send tod en all ju
sed alliday to see da
all allt se la, ehh

<hook>
woo, ooh, ooh
woo, ooh, ooh

<bridge>
allt sem, woo, ooh, ooh
doo, ooh, ooh, sem
en semm alay, ahh, oow, oh
allt sem all doo, woo, ooh, ooh
ahhh, seee, allt semm alay, ahh , see
Bjork, Amphibian

IMAGINE BEING A SOBER GITTE NIELSON

The next day Oz sends me a series of links to places he hasn't gone to yet, in case I want to go out tonight. He himself is not going anywhere tonight. One of the suggestions is a place called "Nowhere"; it's located in a basement somewhere in the city center. There are also a few new places in the business district, probably all posh, expensive and uninteresting.

"It's my post-childhood friends who all go there. I don't have contact with them anymore, they're all ambient and alternative now. What are you then? More or less normal. More or less. What are you doing? Reading Kerouac, for the first time. First time? The Road? Seriously? That's kind of embarrassing. I hope you at least didn't see the movie first. I haven't. Ok. Have to go, am watching *Buffy* and want to return to it. I hope you didn't read the book first...This is a drunken conversation and we're not even drunk...Will call you tomorrow".

Hours, days, weeks later. It's taken a long time to convince Oz to come by my apartment. We've been in touch continuously all day, online, texting, calling, and he has repeatedly made it clear that although he might come by after work he would really prefer to just go home. Really. Although he would sort of like to see Queenie, who's visiting and staying at my place. Still, even as he leaves his office and is on his way, he calls me to let me know that he might not be on his way. But he ends up arriving, much to my surprise. "I'm not sure what to do with myself", he says after entering, "it's been years since I went to somebody's house after work on a weekday". He asks for a cigarette. I offer him a drink; Queenie and I have already had a few. He declines, but after a while he pours himself one anyway while he and Queenie update each other on their respective lives. The atmosphere is a bit dreary. "This must be how Gitte Nielson feels when she's sober", a voice dryly notes. I put on another Morrissey song. Oz suggests a live-version of *Bigmouth Strikes Again*, after which we turn to "Christian Dior" and then watching *Hedgehog in the Fog* as Queenie has never seen it. We stare in silence at the scared hedgehog exploring the unknown territories of the foggy landscape, and then we watch Bjork's *Human Behaviour* in order to compare the visual styles, and then we watch Bjork crying and singing on the gallows as she is executed in *Dancer in the Dark*. The atmosphere remains a bit dreary. Oz types something into You Tube and suddenly Black Lace's *Agadoo* bursts from the speakers and we're watching people in fruit costumes dancing. "People don't know I have this side", Oz laughs, "they think that deep inside I'm depressed, but deep inside there is also this". We do a string of Moldanazar songs, and a string of final songs before Oz will really have to go home. And a string of very last drinks and very last cigarettes.

As I wake up the next morning, I find that Oz has deleted me on Facebook.

DECADENT CITY

There's a gallery opening at 7 p.m. I don't know either the artist or anyone who's going, but it's within walking distance from my apartment so I decide to drop by. Just as I enter the street, someone calls out my name. It's young Vito, who is with his girlfriend and a foreign photographer who I haven't met before. Vito is immaculately dressed, white polo t-shirt, navy blue shorts, sunglasses and slick shoes. He asks if I'm coming to the concert tonight; I say that I don't know which concert he's referring to. It's a band that dismantled 10 years ago but they got back together and are playing their first concert this evening. It's *the* concert. He also asks if I'm coming tomorrow; I say that I don't know what he's referring to. The Sunday flea market of course. *The* place to be. I say yes, sure, I'll come by. Will he be there? Of course! Although probably a bit late in the afternoon; they've been by the lake all day and got sunburned so they won't come before there's a bit of shade. Why am I not wearing the piece of jewellery that I bought from him last time? I do every day, just not today. Is he coming to the opening at 7? Which opening? The one about shadows, in watercolor. Of course! That's where they're heading now. Do I want a ride? Sure. In the car he tells the photographer about the nothing-exhibition; he liked it. I ask how things are going at the contemporary art center; is the new building ready? Is the semester coming to an end? He parks the car and excuses that we have to walk about a hundred meters to the gallery. As we arrive a small crowd is gathered outside, standing around a table with wine. Many of them I recognize from other openings or finnisages, and we politely nod to each other. I take a glass and go inside. After 20 minutes I dump my glass in the trash can and go home.

I should call Oz, but I'm tired. The following day, today, now, I realize that I've started doing all the things that annoy Oz about his old friends. I go to all that is new, all that is opening, to the right places, to yet another art project on the aesthetics of abandonment, to the new, the alternative and the ambient, where everyone else is also going, meeting the exact same people everywhere that they coincidentally also met yesterday.

NIHILISM AT THE TEA PARTY

If you search online for nihilist (or nihilist-inspired) literature there are two books that pop up with surprising regularity, namely Lewis Carroll's *Alice's Adventures in Wonderland* and *Through the Looking Glass*. And then again perhaps it isn't as such surprising. For one, *Alice's Adventures* starts with Alice having "nothing to do" and from then on and throughout the two books, absurd and senseless scenes and questions are plentiful. Alice's sister is reading a book in which there are neither pictures nor conversations, which Alice finds pointless, and she is pondering over "whether the pleasure of making a daisy-chain would be worth the trouble of getting up and picking up the daisies".[1] In a sense, Alice finds the world around to be meaningless which prompts her to chase the White Rabbit, an endeavor that sends her tumbling down the Rabbit Hole towards a place that is in fact even more meaningless.

Lewis Carroll, of course, is not the only author having sent a main character on such a mission. That is moving from a state of discontent to an engagement with meaninglessness. There is Mark Twain's short story "The Facts Concerning the Recent Carnival of Crime in Connecticut" from 1876 about a man who is happy to find that he has become indifferent to his aunt's nagging about his smoking. He is so content about this that he wishes to meet his worst enemy: a dwarf-like, moth-covered creature that turns out to be his own consciousness. After a series of discussions he manages to crush and kill the creature thus turning into a man without consciousness, and in a state of "unalloyed bliss", he starts a spree of swindling, arson and murder. And there is Luke Rheinhardt, who lets the life of his main character be governed by the throw of a dice in *The Dice*

Man, disregarding all conventions and forms of meaning, and in some sense finding a form of meaning through that.

Yet despite some similarities, Alice is also much different from these other examples. For one she, of course, neither murders nor rapes, but just as importantly the world around her remains disorienting. Initially she simply keeps going down, down, down. She falls for so long that she starts first talking to herself, then talking to her cat (who is not there), and then dozing off. And significantly, she doesn't find anything solid even as she eventually hits the bottom of the hole. She is plummeting towards a solid ground that isn't really there but rather presents itself as a void-like, incoherent world, one in which she remains in a state of wonder, surrounded by absurdity, a place where riddles are posed to which there are no answers, and non-existent wine is served. Indeed, when crying out "curiouser and curiouser" once being in the rabbit hole she is so surprised "that for a moment she even forgot how to speak good English".[2] And things do not as such become more clear-cut in *Through the Looking Glass*. The title alone reveals this in "Looking Glass" being the Victorian name for a mirror, and then throughout the book we are presented with a series of reversals of the real world; Alice having to walk towards the Looking-Glass House in order to get away from it, and the White Queen bleeding from her finger before pricking it. Leah Hadomi and Robert Elbaz have rightly argued that the narrative structure of *Alice's Adventures* continues to hover "between sense and nonsense, repetition and difference".[3] The meaningless does not bring forth any stable solution; it is simply there.

POST-ARTISTIC BREAKDOWN

This in itself lacks a point. It's here, now and again, but in the midst of fungus often only as a distant memory of purpose; something that has to be done, something yearned for, a grand idea. Now, at this very moment, the incentive is blurry. It seemed more fun, more engaging, when the whole thing was just an idea, just a plan. Now it's just fungus and eucalyptus. Fuck the view over the river. Sleeping would be nice. Drink, smoke, clean, and perhaps I will.

Hours, days, weeks later. Ulrik doesn't care about the art exhibition any more and we just opened the door to the gallery a couple of minutes ago. The room is buzzing for the first couple of hours. Conchita has decided not to do an official presentation; she doesn't really bother, and people seem to be having a good time anyway. Small groups go to the basement now and then to get more wine; some stand outside smoking; some discuss the works or look through the catalogue. Around eight in the evening Ulrik and I go to a nearby restaurant to get something to eat. He doesn't like talking to people about his works, he says. "I'm always afraid that there will be journalists present at an opening, who have questions to pose". I ask whether he's ever satisfied with his artworks when they're done. Not as such, he replies, he only revisits them if he wants to re-interpret them, but generally he's not really interested in them once they've been completed. That's why he doesn't care about openings; they're not really openings but endings, and endings bore him.

The works will be on display for the next couple of weeks although Conchita doubts that anyone will come by to see them. "Usually people only come to the opening, and maybe also to the finissage, if there is one". We haven't planned for any finissage and during the following weeks we take turns doing shifts in the gallery, which remains largely empty. But the night of the opening is lively. Late in the evening most people have gone to the basement, talking, drinking wine, dancing. Conchita is lying on her back on one of the tables, smoking, exhausted.

WHODUNNIT

What makes anthropology, and social sciences in general, so fond of meaning? Hermeneutics is perhaps a place to start. Deriving from philologists in Antiquity and their attempts to reconstruct classical texts that only existed as fragments, hermeneutics was further developed in the Middle Ages as biblical hermeneutics and the interpretation of religious texts, and came to be a discipline in itself in the nineteenth century. A main figure in the latter period was the theologian Friedrich Schleiermacher who established some of the basic principles of modern hermeneutics: that the individual parts of speech can only be understood in relation to the entirety in which they form part, while the entirety conversely can only be understood in relation to individual parts. This "hermeneutical circle" turns the question of meaning into a question of coherence. Within this framework interpretation thus becomes a process moving back and forth between single observations and an overall context; a process that on the one hand is continuous but which can still be brought to a conclusion in terms of an objective understanding.

In the nineteenth century, the social sciences were highly influenced by positivism, and attempts were made to transfer quantitative elements of natural sciences into the social sciences, amongst others the question of cause and effect. However, William Dilthey (elaborating on Schleiermacher) argued that whereas the natural sciences sought to *explain* phenomena in relation to causality, the aim of the social sciences should be to *understand* in terms of the relation between the part and the whole.[4]

Half a century later the question of meaning and interpretation was taken up within anthropology, amongst others by Evans-Pritchard in his study of Azande witchcraft.[5] Evans-Pritchard argued that anthropology was an art form aimed at translating cultures so that their internal meaning would be comprehensible to others. This perception of anthropology inspired Clifford Geertz in his work on questions of meaning, interpretation and text. Geertz held, in a post-modern fashion, that the social world is constituted by meaning, although "true meaning" is not something that can necessarily be found. Culture, for Geertz, was not reducible, but consisted of a constant play between parts and wholes, and the analysis of it "not an experimental science in search of law but an interpretive one in search of meaning".[6]

In many ways this perspective has had an effect not just on how analyses are made, but just as much on how they are written. That is their narrative. As Cheryl Mattingly observes, "narrative offers meaning through evocation, image, and the mystery of the unsaid. It persuades by seducing the listener into the world it portrays, unfolding events in a suspense-laden time in which one wonders what will happen next".[7] Yet as she further, and rightly, notes, "ethnographies offer a double distortion since in many senses they are stories of other people's stories".[8] She refers to Michael Taussig's observation that *"to give an example, to instantiate, to be concrete,* are all examples of the magic of mimesis wherein the replication, the copy, ecquires the power over the represented".[9] The replica here, I would argue, is not just the story itself, but just as much the narrative frame that is being put to use in order to tell the given story. Despite that the theoretical contents might very well differ from it, the hermeneutical principles of coherence and meaning seem to somehow remain part of this. And we might further question whether this narrative mode has taken inspiration from a particular kind of literature that itself represents the coherence sought after. Literature with a relatively clear plot, a beginning, a middle and an end, in which there almost inevitably is a baseline of suspense and release.

This brings to mind the "whodunnit" novels, plot-driven detective stories in which the audience is invited by the author to engage in the unfolding and solving of a crime, involving deduction through the provision of clues. People such as Agatha Christie and Dorothy L. Sayers were masters of the style. There is rarely anything that goes unresolved, or anything lacking meaning, in such stories. But then there is the opposite:

narratives where viewers or readers are left waiting for nothing. Consider here once again Samuel Beckett. David Kleinberg-Levin, in examining Beckett's depictions of hope and waiting, brings our attention to the seventh book of *Texts for Nothing* in which the main character sits in a third-class waiting room of a railway station waiting for a train that will never come. Both here, as well as in *Calmative* and *Krapp's Last Tape*, "Beckett seems implicitly to be challenging us to consider the promise of happiness *after* the Death of God and the end of religion (…) Our problem, our defeat, lies in waiting, waiting interminably for that great revelation, that miraculous event of messianic or utopian transformation, suddenly erupting into our world from outside, manipulating everything to make it all just right. Perhaps not today, but on the day after tomorrow".[10] This is a condition, Kleinberg-Levin notes, that is also found in the works of Franz Kafka and W.G. Sebald. In the latter's *Dr. K. Takes the Waters at Riva*, a man among a group of townspeople, who are waiting for someone from an insurance company, notes how "those in whom we invest our hopes only ever make their appearance when they are no longer needed".[11]

Stanley Cavell observes in relation to Beckett's engagement with waiting without a telos that "suspense is for Hitchcock what faith is for the Christian, an ultimate metaphysical category, directing life's journey and making the universe come clear, and clean at the end. The overwhelming question for both is: How will the truth come out at last? Beckett's couples have discovered the final plot: that there is no plot, that the truth has come out, that *this* is the end. But they would be mad to believe it and they cannot, being human, fully give up suspense. So they wait. Not for *something*, for they know there is nothing to wait for. So they try not to wait, but they do not know how to end"[12], and moreover that "solitude, emptiness, nothingness, meaninglessness, silence; these are not the givens of Beckett's characters but their goal, their new heroic undertaking".[13] One might argue here that this places Beckett within the nihilist paradox that the absence of meaning is always some sort of meaning. Christopher Devenney notes how "Beckett's art is an art that aspires to be ever less, in the extreme to be nothing – only just almost never' – an art of zero". In this resides the paradox that a play, a short story or a novel is always in some sense something; there are pages, titles and words. Yet as Devenney goes on to show, Beckett was well aware of this himself, writing:

> in the *Texts for Nothing* Beckett will suggest a similar paradox: 'all you have to do is say you said nothing and so say nothing again.' The point (…) is that even when saying nothing it must all in the end be something, if only because it was said in the first place, and the only recourse is to say nothing, and then say it again, and again, because nothing, inanity can always be transformed into something. In *Waiting for Godot* Didi remarks 'this is all becoming really insignificant' to which Gogo responds, 'Not enough'.[14]

Consider also the work of Charles Bukowski. As Nick Belane, the private detective not caring much about finding out anything in Bukowski's *Pulp*, thinks to himself:

> people waited all their lives. They waited to live, they waited to die. They waited in line to buy toilet paper. They waited in line for money. And if they didn't have any they waited in longer lines. You waited to go to sleep and then you waited to awaken. You waited to get married and you waited to get divorced. You waited for it to rain, you waited for it to stop. You waited to eat and then you waited to eat again. You waited in a shrink's office with a bunch of psychos and you wondered if you were one.[15]

As Michael Connelly states in his introduction to *Pulp*, "ultimately, that is the writer's observation. That it doesn't matter. Ultimately, we are just pulp. We are simply part of the machinery of the moment".[16] Bukowski displays a great deal of sarcasm in having a private detective, the character or type who usually appears in whodunnit novels to lay bare the facts for the reader, make this observation.

In *The Sense of and Ending*, Frank Kermode refers to Robert Musil's statement of how good it would be if one could find in life the simplicity of inherent narrative order. For Musil this narrative order is an illusion which led him to write his novel *The Man Without Qualities* as "multidimensional, fragmentary, without the possibility of narrative end".[17] Iris Murdoch, in her thinking about form, equally expressed that "since reality is incomplete, art must not be afraid of incompleteness".[18] Michael Taussig makes a similar statement in *Walter Benjamin's Grave*. Drawing on Nietzsche's complaint that we are too unaware of the fact that when we seek to explain the unknown we tend to reduce it to the known, he writes that "we strip the unknown of all that is strange. We show it who's boss, the basic rule of a university seminar. We tolerate neither ambiguity nor that which won't conform".[19] But that something is meaningless or disturbing or unresolved does not necessarily make it any less real.

SILENCE

I looked up just in time to see Phillip bite a large piece of glass out of his cocktail glass and begin chewing it up
William Burroughs and Jack Kerouac, And the Hippos Were Boiled in Their Tanks

GRAVITATION

It seems as if we keep sliding back and forth. And then at other times it seems as if we're going nowhere, or just...sliding, plummeting.

One does not want to leave. Seen from the outside, One has all possibilities of doing so. One has left before, so it wouldn't be the first time. And most of One's friends have left. But despite not really wanting to be there, One stays put.

Another is always talking about leaving, about this being the very final year, or spring, or month here. Another might sub-let the apartment and go somewhere else. Another is in desperate need of something new, somewhere new, someone new. Some inspiration, some work, something else. But Another stays put.

Another Still should probably stay away. But Another Still seems to keep coming back.

One can stop, Another wants to, Another Still is unable to.

VERTICAL FEATURES

In the middle of a conversation with my old friend David, he asks me what I've found over the years, here in this country. He means which "revelations" my research has caused, which new insights it has brought about. It's late in the evening, and I'm much too tired at this particular moment to engage in any kind of discussion of either anthropology or my research. I'm tempted to just say, "Nothing." But instead I take his question as literal and answer, "Oz. I found Oz".

It's not completely true, though; I didn't find Oz as much as I was taken to him. I'm the one who, in a sense, was found. It was by Victor, a close friend of Oz's, in a bar located in a basement, in the city center, in the spring of 2006. The meeting was random, two small groups of friends that very quickly merged into one and started meeting regularly in the months that followed. At some point Victor noted that he actually had another group of friends, more or less unconnected to this one. At the core of this group was a guy named Oz, and around a year after I first met Victor, he took me to Oz's apartment in the suburbs.

"You have to know something about Oz," Victor told us as we drove toward the suburbs. "Oz is…a little different". And this was also my immediate impression of him, which makes Oz a little difficult to describe. His tone of voice is rather monotonous. He does laugh a little now and then, but his main expression is a loud sigh. During that first encounter, he struck me as a man who was slightly depressed, a man whose life could have been different, a man who was perhaps stuck, but oddly also as a man who fully embraced this situation: a man who couldn't be bothered. And what does he look like? Oz is not handsome, but neither is he particularly ugly; he is neither too fat nor too thin; he cannot be said to be too old but was not too young, either. At least, this is how Gogol might have described him, and how he might have described himself. We watched Peter Greenaway's *Drowning by Numbers* that evening, in between sighs and cigarettes. There were no toasts, as is common to the degree of second nature when guests are entertained here. But there was something to drink. And a lot of Morrissey. And a lot of sighs.

Some years go by and I wake up around 11 the next morning. Oz also gets up. We go to the kitchen. Oz pours some beer and soup. We're on the eighth floor and from the kitchen window there is a view over the hills. His grandfather bought the place for his parents some 20 years ago. Before that he and his parents had interchangeably lived with his mother's and father's parents. The first time he came to this place he hated it. The furniture in his bedroom is from his childhood. There are photos of Morrissey, Tilda Swinton, James Dean, himself and a few others on the walls. There's a shelf with books, his computer, a shelf with CDs and old cassette tapes, his medicine and a series of empty absinthe bottles and various small gifts he's received over the years. He puts together a grocery list while we're in the kitchen. He's glad I came, he says; I'm a brother. For some reason I'm one of the only people that he's never deleted from Facebook; a habit he has. He doesn't remember whether he's still friends with Victor, who is now abroad. I heard that he might come back and visit later this spring. Oz hasn't heard anything about that. He generally deletes his friends as soon as they move abroad, no point in staying in touch

Hakuna slowly wakes up. He's handed the grocery list and sent out for food and cigarettes. Oz tells me about Hakuna's past as an accomplished athlete, and how he at some point got into a fight with four opponents and ended up firing a gun at them. He was sentenced to 2 years in prison, suspended sentence though. It was during this period that the two of them met.

Hakuna returns. He suggests that we take a walk in the hills; the weather is nice. Oz doesn't want to. Not at ALL. We smoke cigarettes, have more beer, eat more soup and go to the living room. We watch most of a documentary about Morrissey while emptying a few more litres of beer. Hakuna is bored by always watching the same documentary over and over again, and spends a good deal of time on the balcony. I ask Oz whether he considers himself as coming from an intellectual family. He does; he learned to read at age 3. A female friend of his once told him that he ought to have children so that he could pass on his genes. He doesn't want to though, for the very same reason. And also because he doesn't want to constantly have to worry about someone else.

Hakuna comes back in; Oz suggests that we watch a movie

instead. Hakuna chooses Greenaway's *Vertical Features Remake*, and we stare our way through it. Hakuna offers to make me a Bloody Mary. He also made sure that I was fed during the day, making us toasts. "I think he has a crush on you", Oz remarks. I note that perhaps Hakuna just thought I was hungry. Oz himself has only been eating a few black olives. He puts on some Placebo videos. Hakuna starts playing with some matches. Hours go by. Oz gets a phone call with the message that one of their friends just died of an overdose; he was only 30. Later he and Hakuna get into a massive fight again. Morrissey sings for us.

JOYFUL PESSIMISM

In *Cruel Optimism*, Lauren Berlant explores the aftermaths of the promises that saw the day of light in the post-World War II period in the United States and Europe, and "the historical sensorium that has developed belatedly since the fantasmatic part of the optimism about structural transformation realized less and less traction in the world".[1] Economic growth, upward mobility and political stability were keywords in the political agenda that transmitted particular fantasies of what makes "a good life" in the years following World War II. Yet during recent decades, Berlant argues, particularly since the Reagan era, the present has increasingly come to be experienced as an extended crisis in which such fantasies of the good life have become increasingly hard to realize for a growing number of people. Futurity in this relation "splinters as a prop for getting through life"[2], leaving many individuals and groups to tread water in a world of crisis ordinariness. The optimism residing within fantasies of a good life turn cruel "when the object/scene that ignites a sense of possibility actually makes it impossible to attain the expansive transformation for which a person or a people risk striving".[3] The notion of "cruel optimism" thus conveys the widespread existence of unachievable fantasies of the good life in the contemporary world. Why, writes

Berlant, "do people stay attached to conventional good-life fantasies such as –say, of enduring reciprocity in couples, families, political systems, institutions, markets, and at work,– when the evidence of their instability, fragility, and dear cost abounds?"[4] This is a valuable question. Yet, it might be just as important to ask, "Why do some people not?" If optimism can be seen as being cruel when that which "ignites a sense of possibility actually makes it impossible to attain the expansive transformation for which a person or a people risks striving"[5], then pessimism or negativity could perhaps be joyful when what is *not* sought after or what is *negated* never comes around anyway.

In Berlant's description of cruel optimism, she notes how the impasse induced by crisis may be a question of being that treads water.[6] But sometimes life may not as much be a question of treading water as one of breathing underwater. Berlant herself gives several examples of people who turn away from politics and the political through what she calls "the depressive position," one taken up "by a subject who acknowledges the broken circuit of reciprocity between herself and her world but who, refusing to see that cleavage as an end as such, takes it as an opportunity to repair both herself and her world". The cruelty remains present, however, in "the compulsion to repeat toxic optimism" in the hope that things will be different.[7] It is that compulsion, or that hope for difference, that is lacking in the sphere of joyful pessimism, or in the accepted loss of optimism. Indeed, as Mark Fisher notes, "hedonistic nihilism" is not a surprising phenomenon in the world today[8]. In this perspective, joyful pessimism may even be seen as a continuation of cruel optimism.

Oz and I text each other back and forth and agree to meet up. I stand waiting in the wind. Oz comes out. We walk and Mushu meets us on the way. Sand blows into our mouths whenever we open them. We text each other back and forth.

(S)UN-DAY

I notice some red stripes on my arm as the plane takes off. They began as a small wound on one of my knuckles. But then the lady next to me strikes up a conversation about absurdist theater and I temporarily forget about them. By transit they have reached my armpit. I count the years since my last tetanus vaccine, buy some raki in the tax-free store and go to the toilet and pour it over the wound.

Everything is going down the drain. They seem to have already been bickering for some hours when I arrive. "Everything will have ended before the summer is over", Oz says. He is sitting moodily at the end of the table. Next to him, Conchita is in a good mood. She has a new lover and is contemplating going to meet with him later. That, however, means that we won't be able to go to her apartment and will be forced to stay at the bar. Oz is pissed off. Everyone leaves. At least the stripes have gone.

It's my fault in some way; I should have never introduced the two of them to each other. On the other hand, I never really did. Conchita just decided to call Oz one evening as I was about to leave the country. They had known about each other for some time, as I had been spending a lot of time with both of them, but always separately. On several occasions I had mentioned to them both that they were the kind of people who would either instantly love or hate each other. They ended up doing both.

By the next morning everyone has been deleted. I send Oz a Facebook invitation, we chat a bit and make vague plans to meet during the day, afternoon or evening ("without Conchita", Oz insists) but we never do. It's raining anyway, verging on a flood. Then Sunday comes around. I'm staying at Sahara's apartment and invite Oz to come by in the afternoon. We buy some beer in a shop and dive into early Bjork, and Johnny Marr-attempts at singing a Smiths song. Oz has some comments on the nothing-manuscript, which is almost done, mainly factual stuff that I should consider changing. After a while we go to find something to eat and end up in a restaurant under the bridge. Conchita calls and says she will join us. We buy more beer and go back to my apartment, returning to Bjork and unintelligible words, smoking on the terrasse with the cats, melting into soft chairs, musing over the word "crew" (creeew! kruh! creu! krrrrruuu!), but mostly not talking, digging ourselves a small rabbit hole.

NULL MORPHEME IN-ACTION

"Ø". The Null Morpheme. Some linguists hold that it's useless because it signifies Nothing - a phonetic sign indicating that no affix will follow a given word. Nothing follows.

In his novel *The Road* Jack Kerouac describes a casual encounter with a woman his main character, Sal Paradise (his alter-ego), meets in Denver on his way from New York to San Francisco. They have sex and afterwards they stay in bed together for a while.

> She yawned. I put my hand over her mouth and told her not to yawn. I tried to tell her how excited I was about life and the things we could do together; saying that, and planning to leave Denver in two days. She turned away wearily. We lay on our backs, looking at the ceiling and wondering what God had wrought when He made life so sad. We made vague plans to go to Frisco.

Soon after they part ways. Nothing follows. Two uneasy lovers with a null morpheme in the room. This is a null morpheme that is not confined to the phonetics of single words in writing. This is a null morpheme in action; a silent follow-up to a spoken intention signifying that no action will take place.

"...the things we could do together". -Ø

POSTSCRIPT

There ain't nothing in room 237
The Shining

LAVENDER SUNSET

Some years later we meet again. This time it's at the street where the gallery used to be located, where the nothing-exhibition once came to life.

It's difficult to recognize Oz with his clean shave and impeccable tan. He's wearing a pink Hawaii shirt with bright blue flowers, black shorts and white sailor shoes. His sunglasses are hanging from the collar of his shirt, weighing it down just enough to reveal his chest hair. His smoking-stop has really done a lot, and he's on a strict diet of organic grape juice. He makes it himself, couldn't live without it, he says. Tomorrow he will be flying to the mountains with his girlfriend for a yoga-retreat. They met at his old workplace. He quit that job some time ago in order to become a decorator, and we are heading to one of his current assignments: Conchita's apartment, which is currently being turned into a boutique hotel.

There are equal amounts of foreign tongues and facade colors blending with each other as we walk towards Conchita's place. No street vendors, no cars, no residential houses. Only pedestrian streets, trinket shops, wine bars, travel agencies, waiters trying to lure in customers outside cafes and restaurants, khaki shirts, khaki shorts, sun-hats, laughter.

Renovations have almost been completed, both here and in the next-door church which, having stood abandoned for a good while, has been included in the complex. Now it is mainly the decorations that are left. Oz is in charge. His first idea for a theme had simply been "all-colors", but it had been narrowed down. His inspiration for the lavender-sunset theme had come from running in the meadows outside town. He does that now and then, as often as he can actually, bringing his camera to capture the beauty of nature. And if not going to the meadows, he takes a plane to the mountains and spends a few days at the yoga retreat.

Conchita will miss the apartment, she says, but with the baby coming it would have been too small anyway. In the downstairs gallery the exhibition is about to open; it's pieces by students from the center for contemporary art; Conchita is curating. She's in talks to become the new director of the center: fingers crossed. Sphroti, her husband, will be staying at home with the baby while she works.

Down in front is an ice-cream stand. Hakuna owns it; he's there almost every day, wearing his small hat. He never randomly goes fishing anymore; instead he takes trips to the western part of the country where Gillian and Stephen have built a small house in the countryside and now run a raspberry farm. Hakuna gets his berries for the ice-cream there. Organic.

Oz and I text each other back and forth and agree to meet up. I stand waiting. Oz comes out. We walk and Mushu meets us on the way. The wind has died down. We text each other back and forth. We spit. We still have some sand left in our mouths.

ENDNOTES

PREFACE

1. As a short and incomplete sample, see Silvia Benso and Brian Schoeder (eds) *Between Nihilism and Politics: The Hermeneutics of Gianni Vattimo* (New York: SUNY Press, 2010), William Brumfield, "Bazarov and Rjazanov: The Romantic Archetype in Russian Nihilism" (*The Slavic and East European Journal*. Vol. 21(4), 1977), Karen Carr, *The Banalization of Nihilism – Twentieth Century Responses to Meaninglessness* (SUNY Press, 1992), Conor Cunningham, *Genealogy of Nihilism* (Routledge, 2002), Bulent Diken, *Nihilism* (New York: Routledge, 2009), Joseph Frank, "Nihilism and 'Notes from Underground'" (*The Sewanee Review* Vol. 69 (1), 1961), Stanley Rosen, *Nihilism – A Philosophical Essay* (Yale University Press, 1969), Shane Weller, *Literature, Philosophy, Nihilism* (Palgrave, 2008), and of course Friedrich Nietzsche, *The Will to Power* (Vintage, 1968) and *Thus Spoke Zarathustra* (Penguin Classics, 1974).
2. Andrew Cutrofello, *All for Nothing – Hamlet's Negativity* (Cambridge and London: MIT Press, 2014), 75.
3. Bulent Diken, *Nihilism* (New York: Routledge, 2009), 29.
4. Andrew Cutrofello, *All for Nothing – Hamlet's Negativity*, 74.
5. Bulent Diken, *Nihilism*, 24
6. See for instance Michael Allen Gillespie, "Nietzsche and the Anthropology of Nihilism" (*Nietszche Studien* Vol 28(1), 1999) and the James Buel's classic *Russian Nihilism and Exile Life in Siberia* (Arkose Press, 2015).
7. Simon Critchley, *Very Little...Almost Nothing* (Routledge, 2004), 32.
8. Related examples of this may be found in Michael Fisher's *Ghosts of My Life – Writings on Depression, Hauntology and Lost*

Futures (Zero Books, 2014), Robert Pfaller, *On the Pleasure Principle in Culture – Illusions Without Owners* (Verso, 2014), Ivor Southwood, *Non-Stop Inertia* (Zero Books, 2011) and in Elizabeth Povenelli's depictions of exhaustion in *Economies of Abandonment – Social Belonging and Endurance in Late Liberalism* (Duke University Press, 2011).

9. Stanley Rosen, *Nihilism – A Philosophical Essay.*
10. See for instance Anne Line Dalsgaard and Martin Demant Frederiksen, "Out of Conclusion – On recurrence and Open-endedness in Life and Analysis" (*Social Analysis* Vol. 57(1).
11. See Ghassan Hage, *Alter-Politics: Critical Anthropology and the Radical Imagination* (Melbourne University Press, 2015) and Joao Biehl, "Ethnography in the Way of Theory". (*Cultural Anthropology* Vol. 28(4), 2013).
12. Lisa Stevenson, *Life Beside Itself – Imagining Care in the Canadian Arctic* (University of California Press, 2014), 2-13.
13. Michael Taussig, *I Swear I Saw This – Drawings in Fieldwork Notebooks, Namely My Own* (The University of Chicago Press, 2011), xi.
14. For another example of this approach, and a more thorough depiction of it, see Tobias Hecht, *After Life – An Ethnographic Novel* (Duke University Press, 2006).
15. Simon Critchley, *Very Little ... Almost Nothing* (London and New York: Routledge), 32.
16. Some parts of the text have appeared elsewhere as articles or contributions, but they return here in altered forms, either by having been cut to pieces and spread throughout the text or by having been elaborated upon. These include "Joyful Pessimism – Disengagement, Marginality and the Doing of Nothing" (*Focaal* Vol. 78, 2017), "Waiting for Nothing – Nihilism, Doubt and Difference without Difference in Post-Revolutionary Georgia" (*Ethnographies of Waiting*. Bloomsbury, 2017), "The Wind in the Mirror – Some Notes on the Unnoteworthy" (*Anthropology Inside-Out –*

Ethnographers Taking Note, Sean Kingston Publishing, 2018) and "Conscious Sedation" (*a...issue*, Vol. 4, 2016). A number of people have read and commented on various drafts of the manuscript, or engaged in general conversations about nothingness, nihilism and meaninglessness during the last couple of years, including Sally Anderson, Andreas Brannstrom, Elizabeth Cullen Dunn, Jane Dyson, Tim Flohr Sørensen, Rikke Elisabeth Frederiksen, Katrine Bendtsen Gotfredsen, Craig Jeffrey, Paul Manning, Tine Roesen, Katharina Stadler and Oto Zghenti, and my colleagues from the Center for Comparative Cultural Studies at University of Copenhagen: Andreas Bandak, Esther Fihl, Lars Højer, Regnar Kristensen, Birgitte Stampe Holst, Stine Simonsen Puri, Michael Ulfstjerne and Rane Willerslev. As has been the case before, I owe my thanks to Renee Caleta Meroni for hosting me during a writing retreat during which main parts of the manuscript were finalized. The main fieldwork on which the book is based was made possible through a generous grant from the Danish Council for Independent Research: Humanities. Most of the people depicted in the book appear under pseudonyms.

OUDENOPHOBIA

1. Viktor Frankl, *Man's Search for Meaning* (Rider, 2004), Irvin Yalom, *Existential Psychotherapy* (Basic Books, 1980).
2. Janne Teller, *Nothing* (Anthenum Books, 2010).
3. Dorte Washuus, "Ud af 'Intet' kom den store betydning" (*Kristelig Dagblad*, January 28th 2011).
4. Andrei Sinyavsky, *Retten er sat* (Copenhagen: Det Schoenbergske Forlag, 1961), 33.
5. Michael Ende, *The Neverending Story* (Penguin Books, 1993).
6. Mladen Dolar, "Nothing has Changed". In: Daniela Caselli (ed.) *Beckett and Nothing: Trying to Understand Beckett*

(Manchester University Press, 2012), Martin Demant Frederiksen, "Waiting for Nothing – Nihilism, Doubt and Difference without Difference in Post-Revolutionary Georgia" in Manpreet Janeja and Andreas Bandak (eds) *Ethnographies of Waiting* (Bloomsbury, 2018).

7. Mladen Dolar, "Nothing has Changed", 52.
8. Mladen Dolar, "Nothing has Changed", 56.
9. John Valentine, "Nihilism and the Eschaton" in Samuel Beckett's *Waiting for Godot*. (*Florida Philosophical Review*. Volume IX (2), 2009), 138, emphasis in original.

SUPERFICIALITY

1. Quoted from Phillip Strick, "Tarkovsky's Translations" in: John Gianvito (ed.) *Andrei Tarkovsky – Interviews* (Jackson: University of Mississippi Press, 2006), 71.
2. Nadia Seremetakis, "The Memory of the Senses, Part II: Still Act" in Nadia Seremetakis (ed.) *The Senses Still: Perception and Memory as Material Culture in Modernity* (The University of Chicago Press, 1994), 38.
3. Paul Stoller, "'Conscious' Ain't Consciousness: Entering 'The Museum of Sensory Absence'" in Nadia Seremetakis (ed.) *The Senses Still: Perception and Memory as Material Culture in Modernity* (The University of Chicago Press, 1994).
4. Tako Svanidze, "Pilgrims Seek Miracles at Opening of Saints Tomb". (www.genda.ge, 22 February 2014).
5. Jimsher Rekhviashvili, "Reports of Holy Vision Sparks Mass Pilgrimage in Georgia". (www.rferl.org (Radio Free Europe), 7 January 2014).

OBSTRUCTION

1. Quoted from Walter Nord and Ann F. Connell, *Rethinking the Knowledge Controversy in Organization Studies: A Generative*

Uncertainty Perspective (New York and London: Routledge, 2011). See also Steve Hays, "On the Skeptical Influence of Gorgias's On Non-Being" (*Journal of the History of Philosophy* Vol. 28(3), 1990).

2. Katja Maria Vogt, "Scepticism and Action" in Richard Bett (ed.) *The Cambridge Companion to Ancient Scepticism* (Cambridge: Cambridge University Press, 2010), 165-170.

3. Richard Bett, "Introduction" in Richard Bett (ed.) *The Cambridge Companion to Ancient Scepticism* (Cambridge: Cambridge University Press, 2010a), 3.

4. Richard Bett, "Scepticism and Ethics" in: Richard Bett (ed.) *The Cambridge Companion to Ancient Scepticism* (Cambridge: Cambridge University Press, 2010b), 181.

5. Manfred Weidhorn, *An Anatomy of Skepticism* (Lincoln: iUniverse Books, 2006), 6.

6. Robert Kaplan, *The Nothing That Is: A Natural History of Zero* (Oxford: Oxford University Press, 1999), 1. See also Charles Seife, *Zero: The Biography of a Dangerous Idea* (New York: Penguin Books, 2000).

7. Andrew Cutrofello, *All for Nothing – Hamlet's Negativity*, 30.

NON-LINEARITY

1. Tim Ingold, *Lines – A Brief History* (Oxon and New York: Routledge), 167.

2. Sara Ahmed, *Queer Phenomenology – Orientations, Objects, Others* (Durham and London: Duke University Press 2006), 16.

3. Sara Ahmed, *Queer Phenomenology*, 82.

4. Thomas Redwood, *Andrei Tarkovsky's Poetics of Cinema* (Newcastle upon Tyne: Cambridge Scholars Publishing 2010), 105-106. In the first draft of the screenplay for *Mirror*, where the film was entitled *A White, White Day*, the scene plays out somewhat differently and does not mention any

repetition. See Andrei Tarkovsky, *Collected Screenplays* (London and New York: faber and faber, 1999), 269.

5. Valerie Orpen, *Film Editing: The Art of the Expressive* (London: Wallflower Press, 2003), 2.

6. Nariman Skakov, *The Cinema of Andrei Tarkovsky - Labyrinths in Time and Space*. (London and New York: I.B. Tauris, 2012), 7.

7. Nariman Skakov, *The Cinema of Andrei Tarkovsky - Labyrinths in Time and Space*, 117.

8. Sean Martin, *Andrei Tarkovsky* (Harpenden: Kamera Books, 2011), 33. For similar comments see Philip Strick, "Tarkovsky's Translations" in John Giavito (ed.) *Andrei Tarkovsky – Interviews* (Jackson: University of Mississippi Press), 70-73.

9. Andrei Tarkovsky, *Time within Time – The Diaries 1970-1986* (London and Boston: faber and faber, 1994), 73.

DETOURS

1. Concept and Theory – Tbilisi, "In Support of Campus Studio, Tbilisi" (www.conceptandtheory-tbilisi.com, 2015). Text abbreviated.

2. See Martin Demant Frederiksen, "De Umenneskelige – Ateisme, Meningløshed og Subjektivitet i Georgien" (*Nordisk Østforum*, Vol. 29(1)).

REPRESENTATION

1. John D. Barrow, *The Book of Nothing* (London: Vintage Books, 2011), 6

2. Ronald Green, *Nothing Matters – A Book About Nothing* (iff Books, 2010), 87, 108. For a range of further examples see Anna Dezeuze, *Almost Nothing – Observations on Precarious Practices in Contemporary Art* (Manchester University Press, 2017).

3. William James, *The Principles of Psychology* (Dover Publications, 1950).
4. Gabriele Schwab, *Imaginary Ethnographies – Literature, Culture, Subjectivity* (New York, Columbia University Press), 2.
5. Martin Esslin, *The Theater of the Absurd* (London: Bloomsbury, 2014), 5.
6. Esslin, *The Theater of the Absurd*, 146-147.
7. Esslin, *The Theater of the Absurd*, 110.
8. Schwab, *Imaginary Ethnographies*, 4.
9. Zizek has argued along similar lines in his interpretation of Tarkovsky's *Solaris* that "within the radical Otherness, we discover the lost object of our innermost longing", quoted here from Robert Bird, *Andrei Tarkovsky – Elements of Cinema* (London: Reaktion Books, 2008), 65.
10. Michael Taussig, *Walter Benjamin's Grave* (Chicago and London: The University of Chicago Press, 2006), 97. For the original quote see William S. Burroughs, "The Literary Technique of Lady Sutton-Smith" (*Times Literary Supplement*, 6 August 1964), 682.

INDECISION

1. For a series of examples see Katrine Bendtsen Gotfredsen, "Invisible Connections: On Uncertainty and the (Re) Production of Opaque Politics in the Republic of Georgia" in Ida Harboe Knudsen and Martin Demant Frederiksen, (eds) *Ethnographies of Grey Zones in Eastern Europe: Borders, Relations and Invisibilities* (Anthem Press, 2015).
2. Joel and Ethan Cohen, *The Big Lebowski* (Working Title Films, 1998).
3. Ronald Green, *Nothing Matters – A Book about Nothing* (iff Books, 2011), 95.
4. Larry David, "The Pitch" (*Seinfeld*, Season 4, Episode 3).
5. Larry David "The Finale, Part 2" (*Seinfeld*, Season 9, Episode

24). For other representations of Nothing or Nothingness on TV see Thomas S. Hibbs, *Shows about Nothing – Nihilism in Popular Culture* (Waco: Baylor University Press, 2012).

6. Sarah Green, "Making Grey Zones at the European Peripheries" in Ida Harboe Knudsen and Martin Demant Frederiksen (eds), *Ethnographies of Grey Zones in Eastern Europe: Borders, Relations and Invisibilities* (London: Anthem Press), 182.

7. Sarah Green, "Making Grey Zones at the European Peripheries", 175.

FREEDOM

1. Ernst Bloch, *The Principle of Hope* (The MIT Press, 1995).

2. Tom Lutz, *Doing Nothing – A History of Loafers, Loungers, Slackers, and Bums in America* (New York: Farrar, Straus and Giroux, 2006).

3. Mary Helen Immordino-Yang, *Emotions, Learning and the Brain – Exploring the Educational Implications of Affective Neuroscience* (New York and London: W.W. Norton and Company, 2016), 44.

4. Immordino-Yang, *Emotions, Learning and the Brain*, 45.

5. Lutz, *Doing Nothing*, 30.

6. Lutz, *Doing Nothing*.

7. Julian Jason Haladyn, *Boredom and Art – Passions of the Will to Boredom* (Winchester and Washington: Zero Books).

8. See Martin Demant Frederiksen and Anne Line Dalsgaard, "Introduction: Time Objectified" in Anne Line Dalsgaard, Martin Demant Frederiksen, Susanne Højlund and Lotte Meinert (eds), *Ethnographies of Youth and Temporality – Time Objectified* (Philadelphia: Temple University Press, 2014).

9. Billy Ehn and Ovar Lofgren, *The Secret World of Doing Nothing* (Berkeley, Los Angeles and London: University of California Press, 2010), 221. See also Razvan Nicolescu,

"The Normativity of Boredom: Communication Media Use among Romanian Teenagers" in Anne Line Dalsgaard, Martin Demant Frederiksen, Susanne Højlund and Lotte Meinert (eds), *Ethnographies of Youth and Temporality – Time Objectified* (Philadelphia: Temple University Press, 2014).

10. Ehn and Lofgren, *The Secret World of Doing Nothing*, 220.

11. See for example Philippe Bourgois, *In Search of Respect – Selling Crack in el Barrio* (Cambridge: Cambridge University Press, 1996), Jay MacLeod, *Ain't No Making It* (Boulder, San Francisco and Oxford: Westview Press, 1995), and Stephen Morton, "Marginality: Representations of Subalternity, Aboriginality and Race" in Shirley Chew and David Richards (eds), *A Concise Companion to Postcolonial Literature* (Wiley-Blackwell, 2010).

12. Deborah Durham, "Apathy and Agency – The Romance of Youth in Botswana" in Jennifer Cole and Deborah Durham (eds), *Figuring the Future – Globalization and the Temporalities of Children and Youth* (Santa Fe: School for Advanced Research Press, 2008), 168.

13. Durham, "Apathy and Agency", 151.

14. Paul Farmer, *Pathologies of Power: Health, Human Rights, and the New War on the Poor* (Berkeley: California University Press, 2005).

15. Durham, "Apathy and Agency", 165.

16. Ghassan Hage, "Eavesdropping on Bourdieu's Philosophers", in: Veena Das, Michael Jackson, Arthur Kleinman and Bhrigupati Singh (eds), *The Ground Between: Anthropologists Engage Philosophy* (Durham and London: Duke University Press, 2014), 139.

17. Hage, "Eavesdropping on Bourdieu's Philosophers", 142.

18. Hage, "Eavesdropping on Bourdieu's Philosophers", 155.

19. Hage, "Eavesdropping on Bourdieu's Philosophers", 157.

20. Alessandro Duranti, *The Anthropology of Intentions: Language in a World of Others* (Berkeley: University of California Press, 2015).

21. Hannah Arendt, *The Human Condition* (Chicago and London: The University of Chicago Press, 1998), 9.
22. Arendt, *The Human Condition*, 177.
23. Arendt, *The Human Condition*, 184.
24. Arendt, *The Human Condition*, 177.

WONDERLAND

1. Lewis Carroll, *Alice's Adventures in Wonderland and Through the Looking Glass* (London: Wordsworth Classics, 1993), 37.
2. Carroll, *Alice's Adventures in Wonderland and Through the Looking Glass*, 44. For an ethnographic depiction of void-like existence see Elizabeth Cullen Dunn, "Humanitarianism, Displacement and the Politics of Nothing in Postwar Georgia" (*Slavic Review* Vol. 73(2), 2014.
3. Leah Hadomi and Robert Elbaz, "Alice in Wonderland and Utopia" (*Orbis Litterarum* Vol. 45, 1990), 136.
4. Jesper Gulddal and Martin Møller, *Hermeneutik* (Haslev: Gyldendal, 1999).
5. E.E. Evans-Pritchard, *Witchcraft, Oracles and Magic among the Azande* (Oxford: Oxford University Press, 1976).
6. Clifford Geertz, *The Interpretation of Cultures* (Basic Books, 1973), 5.
7. Cheryl Mattingly, *Healing Dramas and Clinical Plots – The Narrative Structure of Experience* (Cambridge: Cambridge University Press, 1998), 8.
8. Mattingly, *Healing Dramas and Clinical Plots*, 77.
9. Michael Taussig, *Mimesis and Alterity – A Particular History of the Senses* (London and New York: Routledge, 1993), 16, emphasis in original.
10. David Kleinberg-Levin, *Beckett's Words – The Promise of Happiness in a Time of Mourning* (London: Bloomsbury, 2015), 157.
11. Quoted from Kleinberg-Levin, *Beckett's Words*, 287. *Dr. K*

Takes the Waters at Riva is part three of W.G. Sebald's four-part novel *Vertigo* in which Kafka appears as the character Dr K. (New Directions, 2001).

12. Stanley Cavell, *Must We Mean What We Say? – A Book of Essays* (Cambridge University Press, 2002), 132. Conversely, although Hitchcock was a master of suspense he in fact also tarried with not revealing the cause of an event, particularly in *The Birds* where we never find out what the cause of their presence actually is. As Mark Fisher notes, "what the birds threaten is the very structure of explanation that had previously made sense of the world". See Mark Fisher, *The Weird and the Eerie* (London: Repeater Books, 2016), 66.

13. Stanley Cavell, *Must We Mean What We Say?*, 156.

14. Christopher Devenney, "What Remains? In Henry Sussman and Christopher Devenney (eds) *Engagement and Difference – Beckett and the Political* (State University of New York Press, 2001), 146-147.

15. Charles Bukowski, *Pulp* (Virgin Books, 2009), 83.

16. Michael Connelly, "Introduction". In: Charles Bukoski, *Pulp* (Virgin Books, 2009), viii.

17. Frank Kermode, *The Sense of an Ending – Studies in the Theory of Fiction* (Oxford and New York: Oxford University Press), 127.

18. Quoted from Kermode, *The Sense of an Ending*, 130.

19. Michael Taussig, *Walter Benjamin's Grave* (Chicago and London: The University of Chicago Press, 2006), viii.

SILENCE

1. Laura Berlant, *Cruel Optimism* (Durham and London: Duke University Press, 2011), 3.

2. Berlant, *Cruel Optimism*, 19.

3. Berlant, *Cruel Optimism*, 2.

4. Berlant, *Cruel Optimism*, 2.

5. Berlant, *Cruel Optimism*, 6.
6. Berlant, *Cruel Optimism*, 10.
7. Berlant, *Cruel Optimism*, 259.
8. Mark Fisher, *Capitalist Realism – Is There No Alternative?* (Winchester and Washington: Zero Books, 2009).

REFERENCES

Ahmed, Sara 2006. *Queer Phenomenology: Orientations, Objects, Others*. Durham and London: Duke University Press.

Arendt, Hannah 1998 (1958) *The Human Condition*. 2nd edition. Chicago and London: Chicago University Press.

Barrow, John D. 2001. *The Book of Nothing*. London: Vintage Books.

Beckett, Samuel 2009. *Three Novels: Molloy, Malone Dies, The Unnamable*. Grove Press.

Beckett, Samuel 2011. *Waiting for Godot – A Tragicomedy in Two Acts*. Grove Press.

Benso, Silvia and Brian Schroeder 2010. *Between Nihilism and Politics – The Hermeneutics of Gianni Vattimo*. New York: SUNY Press.

Berlant, Lauren 2011. *Cruel Optimism*. Durham and London: Duke University Press.

Bett, Richard 2010. "Introduction" in Richard Bett (ed.) *The Cambridge Companion to Ancient Scepticism*. Cambridge: Cambridge University Press.

Bett, Richard 2010b. "Scepticism and Ethics" in: Richard Bett (ed.) *The Cambridge Companion to Ancient Scepticism*. Cambridge: Cambridge University Press.

Biehl, Joao 2013. "Ethnography in the Way of Theory". *Cultural Anthropology* Vol. 28(4): 573-597.

Bird, Robert 2008. *Andrei Tarkovsky – Elements of Cinema*. London: Reaktion Books.

Bloch, Ernst 1995. *The Principle of Hope, Vol. 1*. The MIT Press.

Bourdieu, Pierre 2000. *Pascalian Meditations*. Cambridge: Polity Press.

Bourgois, Philippe 1996. *In Search of Respect – Selling Crack in El Barrio*. Cambridge: Cambridge University Press.

Brumfield, William C. 1977. "Bazarov and Rjazanov: The

Romantic Archetype in Russian Nihilism". *The Slavic and East European Journal*. Vol. 21(4): 495-505.

Buel, James 2015 (1883). *Russian Nihilism and Exile Life in Siberia*. Arkose Press.

Bukowski, Charles 2009 (2002). *Pulp*. London: Virgin Books.

Burroughs, William 1964. "The Literary Techniques of Lady Sutton-Smith". *Times Literary Supplement*, August 6 1964.

Burroughs, William and Jack Kerouac 2009. *And the Hippos were Boiled in their Tanks*. London: Penguin Books.

Camus, Albert 1991. *The Myth of Sisyphus: And Other Essays*. Vintage.

Carr, Karen 1992. *The Banalization of Nihilism – Twentieth Century Responses to Meaninglessness*. SUNY Press.

Carrol, Lewis 1993. *Alice's Adventures in Wonderland and Through the Looking Glass*. London: Wordsworth Classics.

Cavell, Stanley 2002 (1969). *Must We Mean What We Say? – A Book of Essays*. Cambridge: Cambridge University Press.

Cioran, E.M 2010 (1975). *A Short History of Decay*. London: Penguin Books.

Close, Frank 2009. *Nothing – A Very Short Introduction*. Oxford and New York: Oxford University Press.

Coen, Joel and Ethan Coen 1998. *The Big Lebowski*. Working Title Films.

Concept and Theory Tbilisi 2015. "In Support of Campus Studio, Tbilisi". 27 November 2015, www.conceptandtheory-tbilisi.com (retrieved 5 January 2016).

Connelly, Michael 2009. "Introduction" in Charles Bukowski, *Pulp*. London: Virgin Books.

Critchley, Simon 2004. *Very Little...Almost Nothing – Death, Philosophy, Literature*. 2nd edition. London and New York: Routledge.

Cunningham, Conor 2002. *Genealogy of Nihilism*. Routledge.

Cutrofello, Andrew 2014. *All for Nothing – Hamlet's Negativity*. Cambridge and London: MIT Press.

Dalsgaard, Anne Line and Martin Demant Frederiksen 2013. "Out of Conclusion – On Recurrence and Open-endedness in Life and Analysis". *Social Analysis* Vol. 57(1): 50-63.

David, Larry 1992 "The Pitch". *Seinfeld* Season 4, Episode 3.

David, Larry 1998 "The Finale, Part 2". *Seinfeld* Season 9, Episode 24.

Deacon, Terrence W. 2013. *Incomplete Nature – How Mind Emerged from Matter*. W.W. Norton and Company.

Devenney, Christopher 2001. "What Remains?" in Henry Sussman and Christopher Dennevey (eds), *Engagement and Difference – Beckett and the Political*. Albany: State University of New York Press.

Dezeuze, Anna 2017. *Almost Nothing – Observations on Precarious Practices in Contemporary Art*. Manchester: Manchester University Press.

Diken, Bulent 2009. *Nihilism*. New York: Routledge.

Dolar, Mladen 2012. "Nothing has Changed" in Daniela Caselli (ed.) *Beckett and Nothing: Trying to Understand Beckett*. Manchester University Press, pp. 48-65.

Donwood, Stanley 2001. *Slowly Downward - A Collection of Miserable Stories*. Hedonist Books.

Dostoevsky, Fjodor 2004. *The Brothers Karamazov*. London: Vintage.

Dunn, Elizabeth Cullen 2014. "Humanitarianism, Displacement and the Politics of Nothing in Postwar Georgia", *Slavic Review* Vol. 73(2): 287-307.

Duranti, Alessandro 2015. *The Anthropology of Intentions: Language in a World of Others*. Berkeley: University of California Press.

Durham, Deborah 2008. "Apathy and Agency – The Romance of Youth in Botswana" in Jennifer Cole and Deborah Durham (eds), *Figuring the Future – Globalization and the Temporalities of Children and Youth*. Santa Fe: School for Advanced Research Press.

Ehn, Billy and Ovar Lofgren 2012. *The Secret World of Doing*

Nothing. Berkeley, Los Angeles and London: University of California Press.

Ende, Michael 1984. *The Neverending Story*. Penguin Books.

Esslin, Martin 2014 (1961). *The Theater of the Absurd*. London: Bloomsbury.

Evans-Pritchard, E.E. 1976. *Witchcraft, Oracles and Magic among the Azande*. Oxford: Oxford University Press.

Farmer, Paul 2005. *Pathologies of Power: Health, Human Right, and the New War on the Poor*. Berkeley: California University Press.

Fisher, Mark 2009. *Capitalist Realism – Is There No Alternative?* Winchester and Washington: Zero Books.

Fisher, Mark 2014. *Ghosts of My Life – Writings on Depression, Hauntology and Lost Futures*. Winchester and Washington: Zero Books.

Fisher, Mark 2016. *The Weird and the Eerie*. London: Repeater Books.

Frank, Joseph 1961. "Nihilism and 'Notes from Underground'". *The Sewanee Review* Vol. 69(1): 1-33.

Frankl, Viktor 2004. *Man's Search for Meaning*. Rider.

Frederiksen, Martin Demant 2013. *Young Men, Time, and Boredom in the Republic of Georgia*. Philadelphia: Temple University Press.

Frederiksen, Martin Demant 2015. "De Umenneskelige – Ateisme, Meningsløshed og Subjektivitet i Georgien". *Nordisk Oestforum* Vol. 29(1): 57-79.

Frederiksen, Martin Demant 2016. "Conscious Sedation" in Martin Demant Frederiksen and Katharina Stadler (eds) *A Conscious Issue*. Vol. 4 of *A...Issue*

Frederiksen, Martin Demant 2017. "Joyful Pessimism – Boredom, Disengagement and the Doing of Nothing". *Focaal – Journal of Global and Historical Anthropology* Vol. 78: 9-22.

Frederiksen, Martin Demant 2018. "Waiting for Nothing – Nihilism, Doubt and Difference without Difference in Post-Revolutionary Georgia" in Manpreet Janeja and Andreas

Bandak (eds), *Ethnographies of Waiting*. Bloomsbury.

Frederiksen, Martin Demant 2018. "The Wind in the Mirror – Some Notes on the Unnoteworthy" in Anne Line Dalsgaard, Maria Nielsen, Cecilie Rubow and Mikkel Rytter (eds). *Anthropology Inside-Out: Ethnographers Taking Note*. Sean Kingston Publishing.

Frederiksen, Martin Demant and Anne Line Dalsgård 2014. "Introduction: Time Objectified", in Anne Line Dalsgaard, Martin Demant Frederiksen, Susanne Højlund and Lotte Meinert (eds), *Ethnographies of Youth and Temporality: Time Objectified*. Philadelphia: Temple University Press.

Frederiksen, Martin Demant and Katrine Bendtsen Gotfredsen 2017. *Georgian Portraits – Essays on the Afterlives of a Revolution*. Winchester and Washington: Zero Books.

Geertz, Clifford 1973. *The Interpretation of Cultures*. Basic Books.

Gillespie, Michael Allen 1999. "Nietzsche and the Anthropology of Nihilism" (*Nietszche Studien* Vol 28(1)).

Gotfredsen, Katrine 2015. "Invisible Connections: On Uncertainty and the (Re)Production of Opaque Politics in the Republic of Georgia" in Ida Harboe Knudsen and Martin Demant Frederiksen (eds) *Ethnographies of Grey Zones in Eastern Europe: Borders, Relations and Invisibilities*. Anthem Press, pp. 125-141.

Green, Ronald 2011. *Nothing Matters – A Book About Nothing*. iff Books.

Green, Sarah 2015. "Making Grey Zones at the European Peripheries" in Ida Harboe Knudsen and Martin Demant Frederiksen (eds), *Ethnographies of Grey Zones in Eastern Europe: Borders, Relations and Invisibilities*. Anthem Press, pp. 173-187.

Gulddal, Jesper and Martin Møller 1999. *Hermeneutik*. Haslev: Gyldendal.

Hage, Ghassan 2014. "Eavesdropping on Bourdieu's Philosophers" in Veena Das, Michael Jackson, Arthur Kleinman and

Bhrigupati Singh (eds), *The Ground Between: Anthropologists Engage Philosophy*. Durham and London: Duke University Press.

Hage, Ghassan 2015. *Alter-Politics – Critical Anthropology and the Radical Imagination*. Melbourne: Melbourne University Press.

Hadomi, Leah and Robert Elbaz 1990. "Alice in Wonderland and Utopia". *Orbis Litterarum* Vol. 45: 136-153.

Haladyn, Julian Jason 2015. *Boredom and Art – Passions of the Will to Boredom*. Winchester and Washington: Zero Books.

Hays, Steve 1990. "On the Skeptical Influence of Gorgias's On Non-Being". *Journal of the History of Philosophy* Vol. 28(3): 327-337.

Hecht, Tobias 2006. *After Life – An Ethnographic Novel*. Durham and London: Duke University Press.

Hibbs, Thomas S. 2012. *Shows About Nothing – Nihilism in Popular Culture*. Waco: Baylor University Press.

Hitchcock, Alfred 1963. *The Birds*. Alfred J. Hitchcock Productions.

Immordino-Yang, Mary Helen 2016. *Emotions, Learning, and the Brain – Exploring the Educational Implications of Affective Neuroscience*. New York and London: W.W. Norton and Company.

Ingold, Tim 2007. *Lines – A Brief History*. Oxon and New York: Routledge.

James, William 1950 (1890). *The Principles of Psychology*. Dover Publications.

Kaplan, Robert 1999. *The Nothing That Is: A Natural History of Zero*. Oxford: Oxford University Press.

Kermode, Frank 2000 (1966). *The Sense of an Ending – Studies in the Theory of Fiction*. Oxford and New York: Oxford University Press.

Kerouac, Jack 2000 (1957). *On the Road*. London: Penguin Books.

Kierkegaard (2008 (1843). *Fear and Trembling*. Radford: Wilder Publications.

Kleinberg-Levin, David 2015. *Beckett's Words: The Promise of Happiness in a Time of Mourning*. London: Bloomsbury Academic.

Kundera, Milan 1996. *The Book of Laughter and Forgetting*.

Lermontov, Mikhail 2001. *A Hero of Our Time*. Penguin Classics.

Lutz, Tom 2006. *Doing Nothing – A History of Loafers, Loungers, Slackers, and Bums in America*. New York: Farrar, Straus and Giroux.

MacLeod, Jay 1995. *Ain't No Making It*. Boulder, San Francisco and Oxford: Westview Press.

Martin, Sean 2011. *Andrei Tarkovsky*. Harpenden: Kamera Books.

Mattingly, Cheryl 1998. *Healing Dramas and Clinical Plots – The Narrative Structure of Experience*. Cambridge: Cambridge University Press.

Morton, Stephen 2010. "Marginality: Representations of Subalternity, Aboriginality and Race". in Shirley Chew and David Richards (eds), *A Concise Companion to Postcolonial Literature*. Wiley-Blackwell.

Musil, Robert 2011. *The Man Without Qualities*. Picador.

Nicolescu, Răzvan 2014. "The Normativity of Boredom: Communication Media Use among Romanian Teenagers, in Anne Line Dalsgaard, Martin Demant Frederiksen, Susanne Højlund and Lotte Meinert (eds), *Ethnographies of Youth and Temporality: Time Objectified*. Philadelphia: Temple University Press.

Nietzsche, Friedrich 1968. *The Will to Power*. Vintage.

Nietzsche, Friedrich 1974. *Thus Spoke Zarathustra*. Penguin Classics.

Nord, Walter and Ann F. Connell 2011. *Rethinking the Knowledge Controversy in Organization Studies: A Generative Uncertainty Perspective*. New York and London: Routledge.

Orpen, Valerie 2003. *Film Editing: The Art of the Expressive*. London: Wallflower Press.

Osho 2008 (1974). *The Empty Boat – Encounters with Nothingness*. New York, London and Mumbair: OSHO Media International.

Pfaller, Robert 2014. *On the Pleasure Principle in Culture – Illusions Without Owners*. London and New York: Verso Books.

Povinelli, Elizabeth 2011. *Economies of Abandonment – Social Belonging in Late Liberalism*. Durham and London: Duke University Press.

Redwood, Thomas 2010. *Andrei Tarkovsky's Poetics of Cinema*. Newcastle upon Tyne: Cambridge Scholars Publishing.

Rekhviashvili, Jimsher 2014. "Reports of Holy Vision Sparks Mass Pilgrimage in Georgia". www.rferl.org (Radio Free Europe). 7 January 2014. Retrieved 20 September 2014.

Rhinehart, Luke 1972. *The Dice Man*. London: Harper Collins.

Rosen, Stanley 1969. *Nihilism – A Philosophical Essay*. Yale University Press.

Sartre, Jean Paul 2000. *Nausea*. London: Penguin Books.

Sartre, Jean Paul 2003. *Being and Nothingness*. London: Penguin Books.

Schwab, Gabriele 2012. *Imaginary Ethnographies – Literature, Culture and Subjectivity*. New York: Columbia University Press.

Sebald, Winfried Georg 2001. *Vertigo*. New York: New Directions.

Seife, Charles 2000. *Zero: The Biography of a Dangerous Idea*. New York: Penguin Books.

Selby Jr, Hubert 2011 (1966). *Last Exit to Brooklyn*. London: Penguin Books.

Seremetakis, Nadia 1994. "The Memory of the Senses, Part II: Still Act" in Nadia Seremetakis (ed.) *The Senses Still: Perception and Memory as Material Culture in Modernity*. The University of Chicago Press.

Sinyasky, Andrei 1961. *Retten er sat*. Copenhagen: Det Schoenbergske Forlag.

Skakov, Nariman 2012. *The Cinema of Andrei Tarkovsky - Labyrinths in Time and Space*. London and New York: I.B. Tauris.

Southwood, Ivor 2011. *Non-Stop Inertia*. Winchester and Washington: Zero Books.

Stevenson, Lisa 2014. *Life Beside Itself – Imagining Care in the Canadian Arctic*. Oakland: University of California Press.

Stewart, Kathleen 2007. *Ordinary Affects*. Durham and London: Duke University Press.

Stoller, Paul 1994. "'Conscious' Ain't Consciousness: Entering 'The Museum of Sensory Absence'" In: Nadia Seremetakis (ed.) *The Senses Still: Perception and Memory as Material Culture in Modernity*. The University of Chicago Press.

Strick, Philip 2006. "Tarkovsky's Translations" in: John Gianvito (ed.) *Andrei Tarkovsky – Interviews*. Jackson: University of Mississippi Press, pp. 70-73.

Svanidze, Tako 2014. "Pilgrims Seek Miracles at Opening of Saints Tomb". www.genda.ge 22 February 2014. Retrieved 20 September 2014.

Tarkovsky, Andrei 1960. *The Steamroller and the Violin*. Mosfilm.

Tarkovsky, Andrei 1962. *Ivan's Childhood*. Mosfilm.

Tarkovsky, Andrei 1966. *Andrei Rublev*. Mosfilm.

Tarkovsky, Andrei, 1972. *Solaris*. Mosfilm.

Tarkovsky, Andrei 1975. *Mirror*. Mosfilm.

Tarkovsky, Andrei 1986. *Sculpting in Time*. Austin: University of Texas Press.

Tarkovsky, Andrei 1994. *Time within Time – The Diaries 1970-1986*. London and Boston: faber and faber.

Tarkovsky, Andrei 1999. *Collected Screenplays*. London and New York: faber and faber.

Taussig, Michael 1993. *Mimesis and Alterity: A Particular History of the Senses*. London and New York: Routledge.

Taussig, Michael 2006. *Walter Benjamin's Grave*. Chicago and London: The University of Chicago Press.

Taussig, Michael 2011. *I Swear I Saw This – Drawings in Fieldwork Notebooks, Namely My Own*. Chicago and London: The University of Chicago Press.

Taussig, Michael 2012. "Excelente Zona Social". *Cultural Anthropology* Vol 27(3): 498-517.

Teller, Janne (2000) 2010. *Nothing*. Atheneum Books.

Tomlinson, Matt 2006. "The Limits of Meaning in Fijian Methodist Sermons" in, Matthew Engelke and Matt Tomlinson (eds), *The Limits of Meaning – Case Studies in the Anthropology of Christianity*. New York and Oxford: Berghahn Books.

Twain, Mark 2006. *The Signet Classic Book of Mark Twain's Short Stories*. London: Penguin Books.

Valentine, John 2009. "Nihilism and the Eschaton in Samuel Beckett's *Waiting for Godot*". *Florida Philosophical Review*. Volume IX (2):136-147.

Vogt, Katja Maria 2010. "Scepticism and Action" in Richard Bett (ed.), *The Cambridge Companion to Ancient Scepticism*. Cambridge: Cambridge University Press.

Washuus, Dorte 2011. "Ud af 'Intet' kom den store betydning". *Kristelig Dagblad* 28 January 2011.

Weidhorn, Manfred 2006. *An Anatomy of Skepticism*. Lincoln: iUniverse Books.

Weller, Shane 2008. *Literature, Philosophy, Nihilism*. Palgrave.

Yalom, Irvin D. 1980. *Existential Psychotherapy*. Basic Books.

Zero Books

CULTURE, SOCIETY & POLITICS

Contemporary culture has eliminated the concept and public figure of the intellectual. A cretinous anti-intellectualism presides, cheer-led by hacks in the pay of multinational corporations who reassure their bored readers that there is no need to rouse themselves from their stupor. Zer0 Books knows that another kind of discourse – intellectual without being academic, popular without being populist – is not only possible: it is already flourishing. Zer0 is convinced that in the unthinking, blandly consensual culture in which we live, critical and engaged theoretical reflection is more important than ever before.

If you have enjoyed this book, why not tell other readers by posting a review on your preferred book site.

Recent bestsellers from Zero Books are:

In the Dust of This Planet
Horror of Philosophy vol. 1
Eugene Thacker
In the first of a series of three books on the Horror of
Philosophy, *In the Dust of This Planet* offers the genre of horror
as a way of thinking about the unthinkable.
Paperback: 978-1-84694-676-9 ebook: 978-1-78099-010-1

Capitalist Realism
Is there no alternative?
Mark Fisher
An analysis of the ways in which capitalism has presented itself
as the only realistic political-economic system.
Paperback: 978-1-84694-317-1 ebook: 978-1-78099-734-6

Rebel Rebel
Chris O'Leary
David Bowie: every single song. Everything you want to know,
everything you didn't know.
Paperback: 978-1-78099-244-0 ebook: 978-1-78099-713-1

Cartographies of the Absolute
Alberto Toscano, Jeff Kinkle
An aesthetics of the economy for the twenty-first century.
Paperback: 978-1-78099-275-4 ebook: 978-1-78279-973-3

Malign Velocities
Accelerationism and Capitalism
Benjamin Noys
Long listed for the Bread and Roses Prize 2015, *Malign Velocities* argues against the need for speed, tracking acceleration as the symptom of the ongoing crises of capitalism.
Paperback: 978-1-78279-300-7 ebook: 978-1-78279-299-4

Meat Market
Female flesh under Capitalism
Laurie Penny
A feminist dissection of women's bodies as the fleshy fulcrum of capitalist cannibalism, whereby women are both consumers and consumed.
Paperback: 978-1-84694-521-2 ebook: 978-1-84694-782-7

Poor but Sexy
Culture Clashes in Europe East and West
Agata Pyzik
How the East stayed East and the West stayed West.
Paperback: 978-1-78099-394-2 ebook: 978-1-78099-395-9

Romeo and Juliet in Palestine
Teaching Under Occupation
Tom Sperlinger
Life in the West Bank, the nature of pedagogy and the role of a university under occupation.
Paperback: 978-1-78279-637-4 ebook: 978-1-78279-636-7

Sweetening the Pill
or How we Got Hooked on Hormonal Birth Control
Holly Grigg-Spall
Has contraception liberated or oppressed women? *Sweetening the Pill* breaks the silence on the dark side of hormonal contraception.
Paperback: 978-1-78099-607-3 ebook: 978-1-78099-608-0

Why Are We The Good Guys?
Reclaiming your Mind from the Delusions of Propaganda
David Cromwell
A provocative challenge to the standard ideology that Western power is a benevolent force in the world.
Paperback: 978-1-78099-365-2 ebook: 978-1-78099-366-9

Readers of ebooks can buy or view any of these bestsellers by clicking on the live link in the title. Most titles are published in paperback and as an ebook. Paperbacks are available in traditional bookshops. Both print and ebook formats are available online.

Find more titles and sign up to our readers' newsletter at http://www.johnhuntpublishing.com/culture-and-politics

Follow us on Facebook
at https://www.facebook.com/ZeroBooks

and Twitter at https://twitter.com/Zer0Books